KU-652-326

THE FORMATIVE YEARS

THE FORMATIVE YEARS

A Book for Parents

CHARLES E. LEAHY, S.J.

DUBLIN
CLONMORE AND REYNOLDS LTD.

LONDON
BURNS OATES AND WASHBOURNE LTD.

NIHIL OBSTAT: JOSEPH D. O'BRIEN, S.J.,
CALIFORNIA PROVINCE OF THE SOCIETY OF JESUS

NIHIL OBSTAT: JACOBUS BROWNE,
CENSOR DEPUTATUS

IMPRIMI POTEST: ✠ JACOBUS,
EPISCOPUS FERNENSIS

DIE IA NOVEMBRIS 1953

Copyright by Clonmore and Reynolds, Ltd., 1954

MADE AND PRINTED IN THE
REPUBLIC OF IRELAND BY
JOHN ENGLISH AND CO., LTD.,
FOR
CLONMORE AND REYNOLDS, LTD.,
1954

for
the Thousand Teens who
made this book possible

CONTENTS

CONFUSION

PROGRESS means change, and change causes confusion. Today's parents, in their own adolescent days, went through the period of the greatest mechanical changes in world history; in some ways their children are going through the period of greatest confusion. It is quite likely that some day historians will refer to the first half of the twentieth century as the "dark mechanical ages." But, be that as it may, the mechanization of life, the two disastrous wars, and the decline of religion and necessarily of family life have produced an upheaval of our civilization which has left its effect on all of us.

Modern parents have had to learn things the hard way; but that very fact makes them more capable of understanding the problems of modern youth.

Our own parents tried to protect us from the dangers they saw all around us; but because we thought they saw only one side, they antagonized us. They seemed to have scant sympathy or understanding for the changes which were so vital a part of our lives. It isn't too hard to look back, with a certain amount of nostalgia, to the struggles of our own adolescent years; and looking at the panorama of our early life, we can see that we wanted change to come too quickly, and that our parents were too inclined to oppose some of the changes absolutely demanded by circumstances.

The humorous thing about it all is that children today look at their parents in quite the same light in which we looked at ours. Of course, there is something in every generation that seems to raise a barrier between older folk and younger, between parents and their children. Adolescence is a period of change which affects the physical, emotional, and intellectual life of teens; and the change and its resulting confusion make them see things and pass judgments in a way utterly peculiar to their own age.

Parents, occupied with interest of their own, tend to forget that they went through the same confusion. Some parents never have attempted to make an unbiased analysis of their own adolescent experiences; but unless a parent can remember his own adolescent years, and his own struggles with his own "older generation," he is very likely to be out of sympathy with the present younger generation and its problems.

Often enough, too, this barrier between parents and children gets its start because parents continue to treat their children as babies long after they have entered the period of teenhood. No one can mark the exact minute when adolescence begins. Some people have said that it begins about twelve, but for each child the age is different. One thing is certain, though: it starts before parents normally recognize it. The transition from childhood to teen-age is gradual, and shows itself in many little ways which parents must learn to recognize. All too commonly parents wait for physical changes as a sign of the end of childhood, although mental and physical adolescence do not necessarily develop at the same pace.

Being a parent is not a dull, lifeless job ; it is an active creative career. There are no good part-time parents, nor are there good parents who do not give much time and effort to thinking out the problems of parenthood.

It is a ridiculous assumption that teachers, nurses, governesses, playground instructors, or any other agency can become the understanding and sympathetic guide children need in order to grow into maturity normally. Substitutes such as teachers and social agencies may take over when parents fail ; they may *assist* parents. But their dealings with adolescents are not governed by the personal love that must exist between every parent and his child.

The number of books printed today giving advice on how to raise children, and the number of magazines and sections of magazines devoted to the problem, give ample proof that parents are interested in a better understanding of the problems of today's children.

A great number of the books are printed with scientific charts that will take the child, presumably, from the cradle to the voting booth with the minimum amount of effort for parent and child. This is not that kind of book.

Some months ago, I visited a family with two teen-age youngsters.

"This is our first experience raising a family," their dad said as the door closed behind them on their way to play tennis, "and it will be our last. And still we are expected to know how to do it correctly."

"There are a lot of books which could help you," I said.

"I've read a round dozen of them," he said flatly. "I bulge with charts. Father, why don't you write one?"

"A priest has a lot of experiences," I said with a smile, "but raising a family isn't one of them."

"Well, you've been with kids a long time," he said. "You should have learned something about them in thirty years. Why don't you have them write the book?"

And that was how this book started. It is a book which seeks to let other parents and other teens try to give an answer on the problem of raising Teen. Actual experiences show how average teens react in typical teen-age situations. Juvenile delinquents and exceptional teens are not the subjects under consideration; the book deals with the average teens and with all of the lovable mischief and goodness that is a part of them.

It is neither a complete treatise on teen-age, nor a scientific study; rather it is a book of the thoughts and experiences gathered by one man, a priest, who has spent most of his life with high school youngsters. This man is still working with high school youngsters, and prays that God will give him the grace to keep in that work until he dies.

Bellarmine College Preparatory
San Jose, California

ALL ABOARD

TEEN-AGE is that short period of transition from childhood to adult life during which teens, while living under the authority of their parents, must learn to live without that guiding authority.

You don't wait until train time to pack a Teen's bag.

There is no other intelligent way of considering the problems of teen-age youngsters and their parents ; and though the thought may not be a pleasant one, parents must regard teen-age primarily as a preparation for saying good-bye to home and to family. Parents, naturally, want to put off considering farewells as long as possible. For, when their teens say good-bye, parents feel that a part of themselves has gone ; and that is literally true.

But in fairness to the teens they love so much, good parents do consider the unpleasant fact, and make due preparations. They cannot wait until Teen is eighteen to teach him things he should have learned at fourteen. They know from personal experience what qualities people need when they start to face life alone ; and from the very start of teen-age they must help their child in the formation of those qualities.

The best way to start a consideration of Teen

is to check on the various gifts he has. The Creator has given all teens an intellect and a will; to each one He has given talents and a disposition peculiar to himself. Teens must become conscious of these gifts, and they must learn how to use them. They should learn directly from their parents, for parents receive directly from God the commission to teach their children. Church, State, School, have the obligation to *assist* parents, not to *supplant* them. The authority of parents is God-given; it must be used in a way calculated to make teens respect authority, not to make them fear or despise it; for their future freedom from parental authority does not mean freedom from the authority of social life nor of the State nor of God.

The authority of God is exercised over younger children and teens by their parents; over adults, by legitimate officials—civil and religious. Teens who are allowed to do as they please without regard for this authority of parents, State, and God are heading toward juvenile delinquency; a juvenile delinquent is a young person who imitates certain adult vices without the cleverness, money, or prestige to get away with it. Disregard for the authority of God in His civil, religious, and parental representatives leads to delinquency in both teens and adults.

Actually juvenile delinquents are less blameworthy for their mistakes and faults than adult criminals; and teen-agers are less blameworthy for their mistakes than adults. As any parent knows from experience, adjusting one's self to life is no easy task. Life is too complicated. The training of teens, then, must comprise many elements. God's authority was mentioned first because it is the foundation of an orderly life.

Teens make mistakes, and they repeat the same mistakes over and over again; but this repetition of errors does not mean that teen-agers are malicious or that their parents are failures. Teens need time, and plenty of it, while going through the process of learning to use their intellect, will, and talents. The time element in the training of teens should be one of the most consoling factors to the good parent; it will naturally be a source of discouragement to parents who refuse to understand that slow progress is normal.

The pattern of teen-age is essentially the same as the pattern parents have watched in childhood. The applications of the pattern will vary; but it is quite amazing how the pattern of dealing with a teen-ager and of dealing with a child remain essentially the same. Take as an illustration the pattern of the first twelve years of a child's life.

First was the *automat stage.* It was a month after little Billy started feeding himself. He dipped both hands into his food and spread it over everything—practically everything, that is, except his mouth. He got some of the food into his mouth, of course, but not very much. Use a spoon? Not Billy. He liked to hear the spoon clatter on the floor. It took a long time to persuade him to use a spoon ; it was as hard to keep a spoon in his hands as it was to keep a knife or fork out of them. He learned, but it took time.

Then there was the *thumb stage.* Billy now sat at the table and was given a knife and fork. After one or two attempts to imitate grown ups he found that knife and fork slowed him down too much ; he compromised on a spoon and his thumb. During this stage he would never think of soiling a napkin. He licked his fingers ; or he might, on specially good behaviour, wipe them on the bread. But he finally got to where it was quite safe to let him go to a party. It took time.

The *acquisitive stage.* This was the time when he took, merely *took,* what he wanted ; it actually wasn't stealing. With help he learned his first lesson in morality, in respect for the rights of others. Did he really learn it ? Did he grasp the fact that God commands him to respect the rights of others ? Or did he just learn not to get caught ? We'll know when we see him in business and politics.

Lastly, there is the *door-banging stage.* Unfortunately, it extends over into teen-age. The motto seems to be, " Anything that can be done can be done noisily." There are other marks too. Billy comes home from school on a rainy afternoon, tracks through the front room, drops his books in a corner, trips his sister, hangs his coat on the floor, teases the baby; and before mother can say a word about slamming the front door he asks for something to eat.

Finding the key to the teen-age puzzle should be a simple matter for parents who have watched children go through the various stages of childhood. Teen is simple going through stages proper to the transition from childhood to maturity, from irresponsibility to responsibility, from dependence to self-reliance.

New interests, broader contact with life, varied and often contradictory points of view flash before Teen with startling rapidity. If he has his parents confused, the reason is that life has *him* confused. At one time a knife and fork confused him. When he came to table he had a definite set purpose, and only one purpose. His fingers were the most efficient instruments to accomplish his purpose. From his own point of view he was completely correct. In time he learned that there was more to correct behaviour than getting food to his inner man, and with practice he learned how to use a knife and fork.

Bill now makes some good choices and some bad choices. He makes choices with his *mind;* and if parents will influence Billy's choices, they must know what is going on in his mind. There is only one way you can find out what is going on in a man's mind, or in a teen's mind: you must have his confidence.

Far too many parents believe that having a

child means that they have that child's love and confidence. Nothing could be further from the truth. Confidence must be won by long and devoted attention and care and love. Many things, even small things, can destroy it, as we all know from daily experiences. But with a teen, over every other destroying influence is the charge of unfairness. In his vocabulary the words "confidence" and "unfair" have never marched side by side.

"DON'T FENCE ME IN!"

DON'T *Fence Me In*! was the title of a popular song once made famous by Mr. Bing Crosby. The title was catchy, because those four little words echo the sentiments of every person from childhood to the grave. The cowboy in the song wants lots of land and a cayuse; and he is willing to forego a good many other things for the sake of this main desire. Any old person, no longer able to adapt himself to changing conditions, prefers poor food, loneliness, and neglect in his infirmities to a home or institution that fences him from freedom.

Teen's parents rejoice that they are past twenty-one, that they are citizens of a free country. They are glad in their freedom, and make many sacrifices to stay free. Though it increases their burden of taxation, they are willing to give even a criminal the right to appeal from one court to another so there may be protection from "fencing-in" which is out of proportion to the crime committed.

Too often when Teen's heart sings, "*Don't fence me in*," he is branded bold or rebellious. I was talking to a young girl, a teen during wartime.

"What do young people think of their parents today?" I asked her.

"Parents don't keep up with their children," she answered. "We and our parents have too little in common. That was true before the war, but the break between them is still greater now. During the past five years the youngster of sixteen is really in the early twenties."

"Well, would you call that the parents' fault?" I asked.

"No," she said, "not entirely. The young people are too stubborn. Even when we are wrong we won't admit it."

"Why?"

"I don't know."

"There must be some remedy," I said. "If you were in a position to do something about it, where would you start?"

"I still don't know," she said.

"How about more discipline?" I asked. That was obviously suggesting a solution, and the response to it was hesitant. "Look," I said, "what is bothering you right now is not the fact that more discipline is needed; you don't see how the young people could be brought to submit even to the discipline they have now. Right?

"Two things are *out*," she said definitely: "The kids won't stand for preaching; and they won't stand for more regulations or for more severity in enforcing them."

"Well, what are we going to do?" I asked.

"I honestly don't know, and I wish I did because some day I am going to have my own children. There must be some answer some place."

Another teen during wartime stated his views very briefly.

"My father is dead," he said flatly. "When my brother was home he used to bat my ears down when I didn't obey my mother. Now he is in the service, and I do as I please."

"What about the Ten Commandments?" I asked.

"I'll have to get used to that idea," he said. "This is the first time I was in a school like this, and there are lots of things I don't understand. So long as I could get away with doing what I wanted I thought I was O.K."

Now let's review the situation. Billy, as a baby, had no judgment. He wandered all over the neighbourhood, into the fish pond, or almost under the wheels of a truck. So his parents fenced him in with a play pen and provided a box of sand and some toys. He outgrew his pen. He became physically strong enough to climb out; and in doing so he said very emphatically, "Don't fence me in!"

Since his mental development kept pace with his body, his parents had to discover a new type of fence: they administered little spankings to his bare bottom. For a while this new fence was very effective.

As his understanding increased, spankings became fewer. His failures to obey were punished by withdrawing certain privileges ; he was taught self-control by the granting of other privileges in return for the voluntary sacrifices required by obedience.

" Billy, you cannot go to the movies this afternoon. Your father left word that you were to mow the entire lawn, and you didn't do it."

Or another time, his mother said, " Billy, if you finish cleaning the cellar this morning you may go to the movies this afternoon."

And then suddenly (the change didn't seem so sudden to his parents ; as a matter of fact they saw no difference) he was no longer a child. He wasn't twenty-one either. The great, and often tragic, mistake of parents is keeping Teen a child or making him a man when he is neither. He is Teen. Just who is responsible if he objects to being treated as if he were a child ? Who can blame him if he falls short of being an adult ?

On Friday, the seventeenth, during his eleventh year of life, Billy does not acquire a new outlook on life, nor does he make a revised estimate of his parents. Although important changes take place in him between the years of ten and eighteen, when he first comes into teen-age his attitude toward his parents is the same attitude he had the day or week or month before. His inclination is to be proud of his parents, to love them, to trust them, even to impose on their love. But during teen-age he begins to substitute for more or less blind hero worship a new and more rational appraisal of the man and woman who are his parents.

Teen is impressionable. He is an idealist who is beginning to reason about persons and things that appeal to his loyalty ; he is greatly swayed by love, anger, hatred, and other passions. To a great extent his opinion of his parents is conditioned by the *fences* they put around him.

Teen-age fences must be reasonable ; they must be reasonable in fact and reasonable in Teen's own judgment ; and they must be adapted to the stage of his development—a constantly changing status of his teenhood. As a child he climbed over the fence of his baby's pen ; as teen, he is not average if he does not jump a childhood fence. He must have teen fences ; and he must understand why they are necessary.

One day after school I found the right time and place to speak to a certain lad ; he hadn't exactly caused trouble in class, but his attitude was constantly antagonistic.

" You don't like my class, Tom," I said. " You don't like the way it is conducted ; in fact, I'm pretty sure you dislike me personally."

He was taken by surprise, but wasn't confused. He was an older boy who had come into a lower class for one subject. I tried to show him that the class had to be conducted in a manner suitable for the younger boys who were regular members of the class. The part I want to get at is this: he denied that he disliked me personally.

"If you don't dislike me personally," I said, "then you must dislike me because I represent authority."

He took me by surprise and admitted that this was true. Then he volunteered further details about his strong feelings of rebellion and anger.

"I'm like my father, stubborn," he said slowly. "He gives me all kinds of orders. He's hard and stubborn in trying to make me obey. That just makes me more stubborn, and I have just as mean a temper as he has. So we fight all the time."

"Wait a minute, pal," I said. "Reason this thing out. Somebody has to be in charge of the class. You'd expect people to obey if you had charge of it. You're in the Boy Scouts if I remember correctly. What do you do about them?

"I make them obey me when we are out on a hike," he said slowly, "but what can I do about myself? I know that even after this talk I'm going to feel the same as I ever did."

It was perfectly obvious that his dad had not constructed a *fence* of the kind that would hold him. "But," says an exasperated parent, "just what fences can be constructed for teen-agers?"

I've thought of that problem often. The play pen for the baby is almost universally the perfect fence for the baby. But as a child gets older, the fences must be tailor-made—they can't be bought wholesale; and they can't be constructed according to any set formula.

The perfect fence for a teen-age youngster must be engineered by parents and Teen working together.

And if the reason for the fence is made clear, the average youngster will gladly help in the construction of his own fence. The actual fact of the matter is—and it can be attested to by any conscientious teacher—that often teens build fences which are too rigid, fences which must be modified by the greater wisdom of a more mature person.

I did my best to point out to the lad I was talking to that his stubbornenss was his best asset—provided he directed it along proper channels; that his final goal was control of his anger and rebellion; and that a victory over stubbornness and anger would take a long time. Then I tried to outline the individual stages of a campaign to which, in definite order, he should give his attention.

Every adult who is not a pest or worse to his fellow citizens knows that laws are needed to protect rights, and knows that social customs are needed to protect the feelings of other members of society. Voluntary acceptance of these adult fences assures justice and happiness for the community.

Teen, while he is a teen, can learn this principle

and can begin forming the habit of acting according to it; but he will do so only after he is mentally convinced of the necessity. Some fences are needed for a teen-ager personally; others are necessary for the common good, and deserve respect because authority responsible for right order demands his co-operation. Society demands his voluntary acceptance of these fences.

Teens use certain brief expressions which give a world of information about their attitude toward fences.

"*It ain't fair*!"

When teens say that, it makes little difference whether the particular fence is really unjust, or whether they incorrectly think so. The effect on them is the same. Even when they submit, the advantage is only temporary, and they begin to ignore or suspect all fences. They begin to look on authority as an enemy which threatens their freedom. They know they can't take the steering wheel away from their parents; so they put their foot on the gas, press down harder and harder, and let the parents try to figure out the steering. Too often this ends in a crash.

By a strange paradox their cry, "*It ain't fair,*" comes not from a bad quality, but from one of their best qualities, their very strong sense of justice. They have other expressions, too.

"*How come?*"

With all their confused thinking, teens can

be very logical about many things.

"Aw, Mom, I don't want to go to church. Dad doesn't." The teen who said that is a man now; but he remembers his words and the reason for them. It was Sunday morning. His father who prided himself on the strict upbringing he was giving his children was still in bed; he should have been in church himself. Teen's mother could not defend her husband; she could only urge her boy to live up to his own obligations to God. Her gentle reasoning and, above all, her good example, prevailed.

But as that man said to me, "Long before I left home I lost all respect for my father. His authority meant nothing to me. I felt that if he could do as he pleased, so could I."

Teens do not expect their parents to be perfect; but they do expect them to be *consistent.* If parents ignore, rebel against, or ridicule authority, they may expect their teens to imitate them; it will be a very natural step for the teen-ager to ignore the authority of his parents.

Teens are more fair and more forgiving than some might think. It is one of the beautiful traits of childhood which they retain. When their parents honestly try to live up to obligations, and are honestly sorry when they fail, teens do not find it difficult to follow parental teaching and example.

But they are shrewd observers, and little or nothing escapes them. No fence can hold them

WINNING TEEN'S CONFIDENCE

WHENEVER people discuss teens, someone always remembers Father Flanagan's dictum that there is no such thing as a bad boy. Father Flanagan spoke of youngsters who have made a mess of things. How much more true it must be of average teens living in average homes.

The mother of several children once came to ask my help for one of her teens. She knew that children of the same family differ very much in character ; but this child was so different that she felt there must be something wrong with him. At the end of our talk, I suggested that she go home and write down all of the things about her youngster that were really bad. She found a few minor faults and many things that annoyed her but not one really serious fault, and some extraordinarily good qualities. The balance was all in the favour of the teen. As a result, she saw him in a new light.

" My parents are too old-fashioned " !

Why do some teens say that of their parents ? Parents should know. They said, or thought it, of their own parents. They said it because it was partly true ; and teens of today say it because it is partly true. That is another way of saying that many parents do not fully understand

Teen's point of view; and when they do not understand his point of view, they do not get his confidence. Perhaps his point of view is wrong; even if it isn't wrong, there still may be a better one. Perhaps he will change his point of view later on. Yet none of these possibilities is under consideration right now. *The foundation for gaining Teen's confidence is an understanding of his point of view—whatever it may be at any given time.* It is no easy task.

So many changes are taking place in his mind as well as in his body that it is virtually impossible for him to adjust himself to his parents' points of view. During this one time of Teen's life it is essential that parents temporarily ignore their own adult convictions, and strain to understand him.

To do this, parents must keep their hearts young. They must relive their own youth so that they can grow up with their teens, and recognize the new aspects under which life presents itself to the present generation.

Next, parents must be in sympathy with teens, all of whom are not influenced in exactly the same way by the age in which they live. Each is an individual with personal dispositions, talents, and inclinations which influence his reactions.

To be *in sympathy with* does not necessarily mean to *agree with* in one's own mind. Teen has a reason for the attitude he takes. To him it is a good reason, and he is ready to hold on to and defend his position. When parents are in sympathy with Teen they have a better chance to understand his reasons. Usually they can find that he is partly right, can agree with him in that, and can lead him on to see the part of his activity which is wrong.

Resentment, or any strong feeling, builds up prejudice in Teen's mind, just as it does in the mind of an adult. Too often youngsters seek outsiders for counsel merely because they resent the lack of sympathy shown them by their parents.

The lunch period at school had just ended. As the boys filed into class, one youngster stopped at my desk and looked up at me.

"Good-bye, Father," he said, "I'm leaving school."

"Wait a minute," I replied. "What's all this"?

He hesitated a moment, then blurted out, "The principal assigned me a punishment for something I didn't do. I wouldn't take it. And he told me to take it or leave school. I'm leaving."

I didn't know the whole story, but I did know enough to realize that the boy was probably right. Actually, nothing could be gained by my interfering. Yet leaving school in this manner was more harmful to the boy than taking the punishment.

"Teen," I said slowly, "it isn't my place to judge between you and the principal; but let's suppose you are right and he's wrong. You have your own free will, and it's a strong one. You can assert your rights and leave school. You can also do something harder: you can use your will to conquer yourself and take the punishment. Go down to your desk and think it over, but see me before you leave."

During the afternoon his strained and flushed face showed the struggle that was going on inside him. At the end of class he came up to my desk again.

"I'll take the punishment," he said simply, and turned around and walked out of the room.

Understanding and sympathy must reach what teens *do*, as well as what they *say*. I think it was Chesterton who changed the adage, "Whatever is worth doing is worth doing well," to "Whatever is worth doing is worth doing badly." There is a world of meaning in his change: no teen can do a thing well until he has done it badly many times. When parents think of the first stumbling steps of a baby, they readily agree; but the same truth applies to Teen.

He may be stronger than his mother, and able to run faster than his father. But now he is taking his first stumbling steps in the bigger things of life. These steps are very important. If a parent pushes and shoves a baby, the infant may fall and acquire a scar on his knees that will last well into manhood. A teen-ager's scar may be on his heart.

Teens are proud of their little successes ; and if parents are interested in their youngsters they will receive the full story with all its details. A few words of sincere praise, even for mere effort, are gratefully received by adults, and even more gratefully received by Teen. Harping on faults and failures takes the joy out of life for adults. Why should this approach inspire Teen to greater and nobler effort ?

" My dad is always preaching." Often enough we adults like to talk out a problem with a friend, not exactly to get advice, but merely to get the problem straightened out in our mind. One of the most difficult temptations parents have to resist is to make every little confidence of their child an occasion for a sermon. Many and many a time a wise nod of the head, sympathetic listening, or undivided attention, is more helpful to Teen than a bookful of profound commentary.

Parents who have no time, and those who constantly misinterpret the actions or exaggerate the faults of their youngsters, cannot win confidence. The positive approach from *good* to *better* is far more effective in helping him attain maturity than the purely negative approach of " Don't do this ! " and " Stop that ! "

One of the great obstacles to understanding teen-agers is a marked difference in two children of the same family. And of course this obstacle is particularly serious when one teen has an especially attractive personality or is gifted with exceptional talent. Without being conscious of it, parents can destroy the confidence of their less gifted child. This lack of understanding can leave lasting bitterness in his heart.

I remember a brother and sister just merging into teen-age. They were only a year apart in age, but differed greatly in talents. The girl was a very gifted musician. Friends, neighbours, and relatives talked about her talent incessantly. Naturally her parents were very proud of her, and were generous in their own encouragement and praise.

The hurt feelings of the boy went unnoticed until one day his smouldering resentment flared into open rebellion. Suddenly he dropped the cover of the piano on his sister's fingers, kicked a glass panel out of a door, and rushed out of the house to his father's tool chest where he proceeded to kick things around and to scatter his father's tools.

I don't know how his parents handled the situation, but I wonder whether they realized that their own conduct over a long period of time was more reprehensible than his sudden exhibition of temper. The things he did, one against his sister, one against his mother, one against his father, showed how deeply he was hurt by those from whom he expected love. In a way, his actions were proof of love on his side, for human beings under the stress of strong emotion often try to hurt those whom they love most.

I do know that four people were hurt by his action: his sister, his two parents, and himself. Which one was hurt the most? Anyone who knows anything about life knows the answer. He was.

Sensible parents with a gifted and less gifted child constantly strive to discover some form of activity wherein the less gifted may outshine the more gifted one. They surely conceal their natural delight over the gifted child when it could possibly do lasting harm to a child just as much their own.

There must be regulations governing every family. But the problem of winning the confidence of youngsters is more important than the mere problem of making regulations. Both can be accomplished if the regulations are tuned to the age and the sense of responsibility of the teen-agers.

Regulations should be as few as possible. In many things an explanation of what is expected and why, together with a few reminders from time to time, will prove sufficient.

Regulations should be reasonable. They should be formed in the best way to attain the desired end: and the desired end of all teen-age regulations is to help the youngster prepare to meet life on his own.

Parents should think out regulations when they see the need arising, but they should not speak of them until the conduct of their youngsters makes it necessary. They must constantly show teens that their own failures in judgment or lack of responsibility are responsible for the regulations.

And regulations in one line should be paralleled by privileges in another. Parents must constantly try to remind teens that they will get more trust and privileges when they merit them, when they show good judgment, when they demonstrate a more adult attitude to life.

And finally, regulations must be individual. The same regulations and privileges cannot work as well for fifteen as for eighteen. It is important to explain this to youngsters. I've met literally hundreds of teens who said, " My parents don't trust, don't understand me." Yet if you talked to them, they would admit that their parents had to insist on certain commands and restrictions. After a certain amount of discussion, they'd even admit that their own conduct made such restrictions necessary.

So much of the friction between these teens and their parents might have been avoided if parents and teens held a council of war before the restrictions were imposed. There is more to be said on that subject, but it will wait for its proper place.

There are, however, some other bars to confidence. Of these the greatest is what the youngsters will call the *double cross*.

THE DOUBLE CROSS

LIKE other self-respecting persons, teens consider that violations of confidence deserve the epithet, *double cross.* Actually in this chapter, we shall not discuss formal violations of confidence, either deliberate or those that slip out in anger. Teens learn early never to trust a person who deliberately violates their confidence, even when the person may be a parent.

Because of the position they hold and because of their training for their positions, we expect lawyers, doctors, nurses, and religious persons to keep confidences sacred. Parents are expected to keep confidences sacred because they are parents. Teens don't reason about that; they take it for granted until their parents disillusion them. And after a double cross they are "cagey," as well they should be.

Aside from formal violations of confidence, there are two ways in which teens may be made to feel that they have been double-crossed: if parents punish them or treat them as culprits for something which teens themselves have revealed in order to get help or advice; and if parents thoughtlessly gossip about confidences their children give them.

It is so easy to lose the confidence of a youngster and not be aware of the fact. Once a high school girl asked me for advice about a matter which was actually trivial but had her puzzled. She apologized for coming to me about it but explained that she had spoken to one of her own teachers only to have some other teacher speak to her about the matter a few days later.

"I was sure I could trust that teacher," she said, "but I won't be caught again if I can help it. I'm glad I found out before I spoke to her about something more serious."

We tend to think of the problems of a youngster as somewhat trivial. Since we have already reached the solutions to many such problems, they may be "trivial" to us; but a little jogging of the memory will recall that when *we* went through the same problems they were not trivial at all. So even the most "trivial" of confidences must be guarded as a state secret.

Teens like some people without wishing to confide in them. In that they are like us adults: we have many friends, but few to whom we feel inclined to give our confidence in matters of importance.

Teens love their parents. They may feel free to discuss their problems with both of them, and this is the ideal situation. Parents and teens can talk things over together with mutual understanding and trust, if parents do not presume to mention such matters to anyone else—not even to teachers—without their child's consent.

Often it happens that a teen, let's say a boy,

although he loves both of his parents, finds that he can talk to his dad about personal problems more easily than he can to his mother. His dad should keep those matters sacred even from the boy's mother. No parent who understands human nature can become jealous or resentful when Teen makes a confidant of the other parent.

When problems arise which are of such nature that they require discussion with the other parent, or with a teacher, a sensible parent asks his teen's permission to make the disclosure. And when the reasons are explained, teens usually agree, though sometimes they prefer to disclose the matter themselves to the other parent or teacher.

But a youngster seeking help or advice should never have to say, " don't tell anybody this." They have a right to expect parents and teachers to respect confidences ; and thoughtless talking, even about matters of lesser importance, merely puts teens on their guard.

And why not ? We adults feel misgivings in dealing with professional people who are " talkers " ; we recognize it as one of the unwholesome traits of modern times. Because the priest cannot violate the seal of Confession, and because the lawyer in the courtroom claims immunity for the welfare of his client, we expect them to have such a high esteem of confidence that they can be trusted in semi-official conversation. When one of them, or a doctor talking to his friends, is careless about confidences, we feel that we want to have nothing more to do with him. Parents and teachers hold the same position in regard to teens as professional people do to adults. Teens expect from them a refinement of honour in keeping with their position, just as we expect it from the doctor or the nurse. Whenever I hear comments about the lack of respect for authority on the part of youth today, I wonder how much those in authority have contributed to this situation by their own thoughtless carelessness in discussing teens.

Another thing which merits consideration under a chapter called *The Double Cross* is the treating of something as trivial which a youngster considers important. The thing may be unimportant in itself; actually it may seem important to the teen-ager for only a brief time. Yet the fact that Teen wants to talk it over with his parents makes it important enough to merit attention.

When I was younger, I learned an important lesson from an experienced retreat master. In a high school conducted by a religious order of nuns he conducted a three-day series of conferences called a retreat. So many of the students wanted private interviews that the good Sisters sought to spare his time and strength by excluding the lower classes from these interviews. They argued, correctly, that the girls in the lower classes had no serious troubles.

"Their problems are big to them," he said, "so they are big to me."

After the retreat was over he had to stay three extra days to give all a chance to talk. Was the time wasted? Two years later the same school invited him to give another three-day retreat.

"Sister," he said, "it is too soon to have me back to your school."

"The students have confidence in you; they want you," Sister said.

He accepted finally. The younger teens of two years ago were now the older teens at the critical period of teen-age. With the greatest frankness and ease they made known their problems, their plans, even their failures.

"I talked to you about this two years ago," many of them said, "but I was just a kid then and didn't know what it was all about."

"Two years ago," others said, "I came in to see you just so I could boast I had an interview with you. But now it is different. I need help and feel that I can talk to you."

I put the lesson I learned into every one of my own retreats. Teens seem to sense the willingness of an adult to listen to them. I believe they get the impression while talking about trifles. *If parents have time for trifles, teens sooner or later begin to talk about serious things.* Any of us who has worked with them can testify that he spent a great deal of time on trifles. Once teens feel at ease they come directly to the point about serious problems.

Ridicule is a double cross.

It is a fact that some people are oversensitive to jokes directed at themselves; indeed many teen-agers are hurt by kidding that hurts someone else. Of course, eventually they must learn to " take it " as others do; but it seldom is the duty of a teacher or parent to see to this part of their education. Life, in the form of brothers and sisters and companions, will take care of this detail. Parents and teachers who indulge in "*boobing*" take the chance of building up a barrier which excludes the confidence of teens.

Among the various blunders and ridiculous and mirth-provoking situations that arise in teen-age are some about which Teen is extremely sensitive; about others he can laugh as heartily as anyone. Parents who want the confidence of teens follow the rule, *laugh with them, never at them.*

Laughter contributes a great deal to social life. But polite people strive to regulate laughter by the dictates of good manners. May parents cease to be ladies and gentlemen when dealing with their own teens inside the home? Some things, funny enough in themselves, are of vitally serious importance to the immature mind of youth. Take for example a first date.

Teen was upstairs in his room getting ready to go out on his first big date. Ordinarily his younger brothers and sisters would have had no interest in what he was doing, nor in how long it took him to do it. Tonight they grew impatient because he was taking so long.

Actually they weren't particularly concerned about how he looked when he did appear but, like hounds on the trail of a scared rabbit, they were impatient for the kill. Everyone found an excuse to remain in the front room with the parents.

At last the door opened and a sheepish teen stood in front of his mother.

" Isn't he cute ! "

" Where did you get the tie ! " (Actually it was his dad's.)

" Boy, you smell like a decayed barber shop ! "

Dad looked up from his paper. " Son," he said with a wide smile, " you look as wonderful as your mother did in that last hat she bought ! " Everyone roared with laughter.

Everyone but mother. She remembered the incident of that hat. She remembered how all the happiness of an afternoon of shopping had been spoiled by the thoughtless reception of the family. She'd even cried a bit to herself before she started supper.

" I think you look very nice," she said to Teen. " Come over closer."

Then, as if she hadn't quite made up her mind, she asked him if he didn't think another tie would be nicer. She went up to his room with him, picked out another tie, got off some of the surplus oil, and persuaded him that the black shoes looked better for evening. She sat on his bed as they talked, and they went down the stairs together.

"'Night, Ma," he said as they stood in the doorway, "don't wait up for me." He winked knowingly, and went whistling down the road.

"YOU LITTLE DEVIL"

ONE summer day when all the windows of the house were open, a pre-teen boy and his mother were standing in the kitchen. Suddenly the raucous voice of the woman next door floated in through the kitchen window.

"You little devil!" she screamed at her son.

After a moment the little boy turned to his mother. "Mother," he said, "you never call me a devil, do you?"

It's my guess that the difference between the two mothers was much greater than the difference between the two boys.

No two teens are just alike, for the Creator had given them not only an intellect and free will, but also tools with which to work: talents, dispositions, inclinations, characteristics peculiar to each teen. Parents must keep these individual variations in mind.

The mother mentioned at the beginning of this chapter found that her teen did many things that annoyed her. He got on her nerves; and she hadn't realized that often the trouble was with her nerves as much as with her teen. Constant irritation had so confused her that she did not distinguish between "bad" and "irritating." A person with a taste for music may be irritated because radio programs feature orchestras that blare long and loud without ever blundering into any real music ; but he would be unfair if he let his irritation proclaim that a man is a bad musician merely because he plays in such an orchestra.

Most of the things that irritate parents are not bad in themselves, nor are they a sign that Teen is bad because he does them. The doing of irritating things is simply peculiar to the teen-age stage of development. Some of the things do indicate tendencies which could lead to something bad, and a teen-ager must be taught to correct them, just as the infant was taught to use a knife and fork instead of his fingers.

Teens are thoughtless, careless, noisy, quarrelsome ; they think only of play, of their comfort, of food. They are often lazy in work, in study, and in co-operation at home. Parents should make up a list of the deficiencies of their own youngster. But all the defects add up to one conclusion : their judgment and their will have not developed to the adult stage. They are teens.

Teen faults are irritating in themselves but they become more irritating to parents because of their own physical or mental condition, or because parents have still much to learn about self-control.

A young colt, not yet broken to the saddle, is very irritating. But a good horse trainer tries to bring out the good qualities of the colt ; he knows that calmness and patience get the surest and quickest results. And animals and people react the same way to patience and calmness.

Patience, tolerance, and forgiveness are *musts* for those who would train teens. My authority for that statement is the greatest Teacher of all, Jesus Christ. "Learn of Me for I am meek and humble of heart," He said. Patience, tolerance, and forgiveness taken together constitute meekness.

The world today is in mortal fear of two weapons: the atom bomb, a weapon of destruction; and the Spirit of Christ, a weapon of construction. We experiment with the former and shun the latter. A study of history from the invention of gunpowder to the discovery of the atom bomb should convince us that men never will submit to force. Nations and individuals would rather die resisting. And teen-agers are no different.

The Spirit of Christ is the salvation of nations; and when that spirit rules parents in their own government it is the salvation of teens. From the parents' point of view, this practice of meekness seems to put the entire burden on them. Patience, tolerance, and forgiveness do demand sacrifices, and sacrifices are repugnant to human nature. But unless parents realize that their sacrifices are investments in the success of their teens, they will certainly find meekness almost an impossibility.

Teens can try the patience of anyone. Parents who are naturally calm have an advantage over those who are more excitable; but a conscious exercise of patience is necessary for all parents.

A Reader's Digest article for November, 1945, "Boss Ketterling, The Man who Falls Forward," describes the failures of a successful man in the field of science. Patience in the face of repeated failure is the price the scientist pays for success.

"It's always been that way with every one of our developments," Boss Ketterling says in the *Digest* article, "a succession of failures with just enough success to keep us hanging on by our eyebrows . . . . If only there were a million more boys being taught what it takes to be a researcher, what a world this could be ! Think of the poor kids. From the time they start to school they're examined three or four times a year, and if they flunk it's a disgrace. If they fail once they're out. In contrast, all research is 99.9% failure, and if you succeed once, you're in."

Parents should think of the patience necessary to carry on in the face of the 99.9 per cent failure that brought all the marvellous inventions of our age. Neither the "poor kids" nor their parents are confronted with any such percentage of failure in the laboratory of teen-age.

Parents with the vision of the finished product, manhood and womanhood made of their own flesh and blood, have in that vision their motive for patience during the formative period.

Successful parents are not persons who have some extraordinary power which enables them to say a thing once, and have teens do it correctly from that time on. Rather, *successful parents are those who have the patience to lead teens through a long series of repeated failures until they learn the right way to do the right thing of their own free choice.*

Patience helps parents realize that it is normal for Billy to drag his feet, slam doors, and leave his clothes all over the house—especially when his father does the very same thing. Patience keeps parents' minds clear so that they do not think Billy is rebellious, disrespectful, or incurable just because his training demands frequent and constant reminders. And patience directs parents in their admonitions so that Billy has no excuse for feeling that he is the victim of nagging.

Tolerance means allowance for variation from a standard. For parents of teen-agers it means ignoring some faults or mistakes in order the better to concentrate on the correction of others. It also means making allowances for mistakes in more serious matters while teaching youngsters to acquire good habits.

Tolerance is particularly needed when there are several teens in the same family. One teen may have great difficulty with a situation which another handles with ease. In such cases tolerance warns parents not to hold one teen up as a model to the other, for such comparisons can only discourage or antagonize the more backward teen.

In general, lack of a sense of responsibility is the pre-dominant characteristic of teen-age.

Bear with me for repeating that. Most of the time teens are hardly aware of their failures, even after parents have reminded them several times. Certainly their minds remain unimpressed with the significance of their failures. And Teen's lack of responsibility is always aggravated when parents put the same emphasis on things important and unimportant.

Patience and tolerance save parents from the confidence shattering error of branding Teen's mistakes, due to immaturity, as malicious. The childhood trait of living in the present continues into teen-age ; teens, therefore, are more inclined to act on the impulse of the moment than with mature consideration. When they begin to act with such maturity they are adults ready to go out on their own.

Tolerance of faults does not mean indifference ; it merely suggests a more intelligent method of dealing with faults, a method based upon an understanding of the cause and modifying circumstances of the faults committed.

A young mother trying to teach her baby to speak his first few words is so thrilled with " da-da " and " ma-ma " that she threatens to bore her friends to exhaustion. But when the same child is a bit older she threatens him with a hairbrush to break the habit of baby talk. When baby becomes a teen-ager, tolerance indicates how much to expect—not on the basis of age alone, but of character, disposition, health, and aptitude.

Tolerance breeds gentleness, and that quiet firmness which makes teens stop to think. It is more effective than much talking and shouting. Tolerance, too, teaches parents the power of silence as a corrective for the mistakes of teens. *Complete silence, intelligently used, can be one of the most effective means of training youngsters.*

A teen with whom I had some semiofficial dealings used to take advantage of her visits to regale me with all sorts of personal problems. But, as a blind man could easily see, she was seldom completely honest with her facts. She was like a patient who fears the doctor's verdict if he knows all the symptoms. One day she left my office, and in a very few minutes returned.

" I wanted to tell you that I lied to you a few minutes ago," she said.

" I know that," I said as disinterestedly as I could. " I've known for some time that you've been feeding me little lies."

" But you trusted me as if I were always telling the truth," she said. " Why ? "

" I had an idea," I said, " that your own native honesty would tell you about it better than I could."

Waiting for the right time to correct certain faults is the most effective way of developing a sense of responsibility ; but that is possible only when parents possess patience and tolerance.

Sometimes teens do realize, and are willing to admit guilt of their own accord ; not always of course. Some people simply cannot bring themselves to admit such things. But in matters involving justice, fair play, and honour—according to Teen's concept of these virtues—their sense of guilt keeps growing until one day they do burst out with a confession of their fault.

Forgiveness is the third element of meekness. And as God has honoured parents with a share in His creative power, so parents should honour God by imitating His forgiveness. He forgives us not merely because He loves us but also because He understands us. Parents love their children. If they are patient and tolerant, parents understand their teens; and understanding the *teen-ness* of their offspring, they forgive.

But forgiveness is not indifference or weakness either. The idea of forgiveness supposes full knowledge of the fault, and of the degree of responsibility for the commission of the fault. This degree of responsibility determines the kind of punishment or admonition which precedes forgiveness.

There are many failings natural to teen-age which require explanation, not punishment. The explanation should be given in such a way that Teen knows that his parents understand and are in sympathy with him, but still cannot agree with him. For parents merely to understand is not enough. Teen must *know* that his parents understand ; then he will more easily realize that his parents must be right.

When parents decide to handle a particular fault by explanation rather than by punishment, forgiveness should be complete. But here a difficulty arises. Teens do repeat their faults after explanation—and after punishment too. That is not a sign of malice nor weakness. A trained will is the result of a long slow process. Teens haven't lived long enough to have a trained will. Therefore parents need great patience, tolerance, and forgiveness during this period of will development.

There are teen-age faults which merit more than mere explanation. They deserve punishment. Indeed, a repetition of the faults can be avoided only by punishment properly administered. But in all cases, punishment must be followed by complete forgiveness. Harping on past failures makes teens feel that since they are " in the doghouse anyway " they might just as well do a few more things.

If worried parents would just make out a list of the faults which they find in their teens, they would certainly find that most of these faults are irritating, not bad. And they would experience the relief of happiness that comes from knowing that they are not failures as parents.

One day, at the close of the war, a man was telling me about a grand family reunion he was having. Every one of his youngsters had returned from the war sound of mind and body.

"But Father," he said, "it burns me up the way those kids agree now with what I tried to teach them when they were youngsters. When they were young they made my life miserable, and were in trouble all of the time. I was a failure as a father, but the war made them turn out all right."

"War nothing!" I said. "You're not a failure. You trained them to go out on their own. That is all a good parent can do."

"You mean that?" he asked.

"Of course I mean it," I said.

"Boy! that makes me feel good. Tell other parents that. There must be a lot of them like me."

SERIOUS FAULTS.

WHILE it is perfectly true that many teen-age faults are irritating rather than bad, some are unquestionably evil. And the multiplicity and constant recurrence of minor faults often blinds parents to the beginnings of more serious problems. Too often when they have lost or have never won the confidence of their teens, parents are the last ones to whom teens make known their serious problems.

In any discussion of this sort the word *problems* rather than *faults* should be used ; for the moral responsibility of teens depends on their knowledge or ignorance of evil, and the degree to which their free will is involved.

At some time during adolescent years Teen becomes capable of feeling every physical and psychological impulse to good and evil which we associate with adult life. Because of varying personal traits, environment, companionship, or home training, his response to these impulses is usually centred in one or two fields of activity.

Of course when he has a serious problem, and teens do have quite serious problems, Teen sorely needs someone in whom to confide. He should not have to wonder, " Can I talk to Dad ? to Mother ? to my teacher ? " It should be as natural for him to go to his parents as it was to ask for a drink of water when he was too small to reach the faucet.

Too many parents have a positive fear of the sex questions Teen will ask them. So obsessed with this fear do they become that they spend hours speculating on the form the questions will take, and what they will say when called upon to face the ordeal. They should reflect a moment on the problems they have already dealt with successfully !

There was the triangle-and-talcum period. In the beginning, changing little Billy's diapers was a routine task. When he grew a little there was the struggle to get him to tell his needs in time. No embarrassment about that. And when he had learned the lesson, there was no embarrassment when quite regularly he came into the front room, and in front of the visitors gave audible proof of how well he had learned his lesson. Mother or one of the older children took his hand and walked from the room, and everybody understood.

The next step was to praise him for speaking in time, and then add that when visitors were present he should come to Mother and whisper ; it was not good manners to say it out loud. What family forgets that situation ? Billy walked into the front room, right up to Mother, and waited for her to give her attention. Everyone acted as if there were no suspicion of what it was all about. Mother bent her head and he whispered in her ear.

Then Mother excused herself, and the two left the room together. Finally, he knew all about the matter and took care of himself.

There are so many other natural functions which he must learn: food, blowing his nose, washing his body, decency in keeping himself covered; and also the facts of sex, just as much a part of his physical nature as any of the others. He has a right to know about it. He is going to learn about it either from his parents or from somebody on the street. To fret about it is silly.

A good mother, one who tried desperately to do her duty no matter what the cost, martyred herself with the thought of sex information. One day she was washing the dishes, and her son was drying them slowly, as boys usually do.

"Mom," he said, without a single bit of warning, "where do I come from?"

She almost dropped a plate when she realized that the fateful moment had arrived. Quickly she recalled all that she had heard, all that she had read about the birds and the bees. She started with the flowers and gradually worked her way up, all the time stealing quick glances at him to see how it was registering.

There was no surprise on his face, nor in fact any signs of understanding; he put the dishes down half-dried as usual; he looked out the window with the vacant stare all youngsters assume when their parents are making a long speech. Finally she paused to snatch a hasty breath.

"Mom," he interrupted, "where did I come from? Jimmy wants to know. He says that he was born in Chicago."

There is no such thing as a certain time, or a definite form for questions involving sex. Curiosity in this matter starts well before teen-age, and youngsters ask many questions which are not directly about sex, but are closely related to it. Parents should answer all such questions truthfully and clearly, no matter how trivial, *but only far enough to satisfy the child's curiosity at the time.* Giving answers this way is just as simple and natural as it was to train little Billy to make his needs known when he was a child.

Parents who satisfy the curiosity of their children this way not only prepare them for the further instructions proper to teen-age, but also train them to look for information at home instead of down the street.

A teen-age girl was talking about the wonderful family spirit in their home, and the freedom with which all the children discussed problems with their parents.

"I guess some people would be shocked to hear our conversations about some of the problems," she said.

"Sex, you mean?" I asked.

"Yes," she said. "Most of our questions they answered themselves. And when they thought it was time for us to know everything, they sent us to our family doctor. When we came home we knew what it was all about, and they knew we understood. After that it was clear sailing. All kids ought to be able to talk things over the way we do."

Parents who use good judgment in this matter save their teens and themselves much sorrow. They should be close enough to their own children to be able to judge when is the best time, neither anticipating nor delaying too long. Parents who have a strong aversion to giving instructions themselves may well send their teens to the family doctor. Then they must choose one who is not trying to justify his own immorality by teaching others that certain immoralities are only natural.

Lack of instruction at home and the wrong kind of knowledge gotten away from home have caused many teens to fall into sin. One which is a cause of worry to good parents, usually known to teens by one of its slang names, is masturbation. Few teens fail to hear about it.

I have used the word *sin* because failures against purity are in an entirely different class from teen-age faults which irritate parents. Far too many books on adolescents treat masturbation as something purely natural merely because temptations to it are very common with growing adolescents. For them it is "old-fashioned" to think of impurity as sin. The final conclusion you reach after reading their learned books is that decent people are merely people who are out of date.

But there is a standard of morality set by God; and all are bound to conform to that standard. Violations of moral standards are not evil because they shock society but because they break the law of God. The smug hypocrisy of one standard for men, another for women, or what is bad on Skid Row is refined in Hollywood, does not deceive the wide-awake youth of today. Teens have little respect for the opinion of parents or others who ignore the authority of God and explain away His teachings when it suits their purpose.

The only honest and effective way of dealing with the subject of purity is to tell teens the truth. Acts which are sinful must be represented as sinful; and friendship with God is the fundamental motive for avoiding such acts, and for overcoming a habit once it is formed. Other motives soon lose their force.

When his parents find out that a boy or girl fails by self-abuse they must avoid any shock, disappointment, or indignation. To do so may be fatal, for teen is already ashamed of himself, at least secretly. Because his conscience pulls one way while his habit pulls another, he needs help. His will is torn, strong at one time, weak at another. He can overcome himself only with the co-operation of his will; and blame and indignation will not win that co-operation.

Parents must win his confidence. He must know that his parents sympathize with him, and understand the struggle he is called on to make. No parent who realizes that Teen is a human being should find it difficult to understand and sympathize.

Teen has not lost his ideal just because he has gone against that ideal. The fact that he feels shame is proof of that; and often coarseness and bravado are but an attempt to escape the turmoil caused by the fight between his acts and his ideals. Parents give him new hope when they make it plain that nothing he has done can kill their faith in his ideals.

Parents should realize that Teen feels an aloneness in his struggles and in his failures. The fact is that the majority of people have the same or similar temptations. The unfortunate fact is that very many fail, as he has failed. But very many have conquered the habit completely. Their teen might just as well be one of these.

This is preliminary, and its purpose is to make Teen see that his parents understand, that he give them his confidence. But also contained in this approach is an appeal to his intellect and will in preparation for the real campaign for winning the active, voluntary co-operation of his will to do better.

Once on a radio program a rabbi, two ministers, and I were holding a round-table discussion about the effect of modern practical atheism on youth, and what religion can do to offset its influences. Rather unexpectedly one of the ministers said,

"Of course, the Catholic Church has the Sacramental System to make its work effective."

Reception of the Sacraments of Penance and Holy Communion has figured in all my dealings with teens who have fallen into impurity. Not everyone who reads this book will understand the great help offered by these two Sacraments. Yet those who have a faith different from mine should realize that God's help is essential, and should investigate to see what definite helps their own religion has to offer.

Parents, once Teen's confidence in this delicate matter is won, must have a definite plan of help to give him. The plan must make use of the natural and the supernatural; it should be a combination of common sense and the Sacraments.

I once talked on the temptations of sex to the students of a boys' school. After the talk one youngster came to my room.

"Father," he said, "I know about that Commandment, even about a lot of the muck you could not talk about in public. But when I was small I learned a bad habit, and it has been an awful fight ever since. I still fail."

"How often," I asked in the course of our conversation, "do you go to Confession and receive Holy Communion?"

"Fairly often," he said hesitantly. "I used to go oftener, but I committed this sin so much I felt it wasn't square to keep on receiving the Sacraments."

His situation was so typical; and his parents could have saved him so much unhappiness. I praised him for his honesty with himself and with God. One must have sorrow and a resolution to avoid sin in order to obtain forgiveness in the Sacrament of Penance. Then I tried to explain that Christ had made the Sacrament of Penance one which could be received often, for even though penitents have a good resolution at the time of their Confessions, as human beings they fall into sin again through weakness; that frequent Confession stirs the penitent to renewed acts of the will; and that the Sacrament, according to the teaching of Christ, gives pardon and also special graces to strengthen the will against future temptations.

"Did you ever try to pick out some priest whom you trust and with whom you could talk freely?" I asked.

"No, I never did that," he said.

"I've met other boys just as good as you are," I said, "and having the same fight. They used to go to a priest regularly and report their successes and failures. Each time they failed, the priest insisted they go to the Sacraments for the express purpose of conquering this habit. You could do that."

"Did it work with them?" he asked. "I mean, did they get strong enough to really keep away from that sin?"

"Yes," I answered, And I was glad to know

from experience with many teens of both sexes that I was not offering a false hope.

Parents of understanding and sympathy find little difficulty in selecting the natural helps suggested by common sense and a knowledge of their youngsters; but they need great prudence in urging the use of the Sacraments. Confession is not like a service station where you run an automobile in to be washed and polished. The soul is not a machine, but a living thing with free will; and the co-operation of that free will is necessary for the Sacrament to be effective. Parents should prudently urge a youngster to select some priest whom he likes for his confidant and regular confessor. The fight is a hard one, but teens make it with more hope and courage when they have a friend who understands both their problem and their particular character with its virtues and weaknesses.

On the natural side, the very fact that parents remove self-abuse from the category of secret acts by their sympathetic discussion with a youngster does much to help him overcome his temptations. With this they can see that Teen keeps himself personally clean, avoids sensational or suggestive reading and movies, and gets a thoroughly wholesome dose of exercise.

Many of the books I have seen contain treatises on homo-sexuality. I wish there were no reason for the treatises. If it ever should arise, how should parents deal with this situation? All I can say is that I have not met, so far, a teen who was not deeply ashamed and worried, and willing to co-operate in any plan that promised victory. I remember a lad who came to me.

"Father," he said, "there's a boy who gets me into trouble with him, and I'm not strong enough to say 'no.' What can I do?"

We talked about it for a while until I had most of the facts and the background.

"Do you really want to stop it?" I said finally.

"Yes I do," he said, "but I just give in all the time."

"How big is he?"

"My size, maybe a little bigger."

"Are you willing to risk a black eye?"

"If it will help," he said tentatively.

"All right," I said, "the next time he propositions you, don't say a word. Just haul off and hit him. Hit him as hard as you can, and walk away. You might get into trouble if it happens at school. Can do?"

"Can try," he said. And he did.

All that has been said on the subject of the ideals of teens in purity applies to sins of fornication. These sins, if they take place at all, are more likely to happen during the company-keeping period of teen-age. But they require a somewhat different treatment.

Youngsters who fall this way think they are in love, and perhaps they really are. They look upon themselves as grown up and free to act like the adults they hear and read about. Certainly every attempt has been made to give them the impression that the ideal of purity is a mark of childhood. Every time second-rate script writers and comedians are at a loss for something funny they fall back on this theme, and it very seldom fails to bring laughs from adults.

Teens who have succumbed to sexual intercourse do not understand the meaning of parenthood. They have mere biological information. Whether they have received it from a doctor, from their parents, or down the street makes little difference if they do not understand the beauty and spirituality of parenthood and marriage as the explanation of sex in rational beings.

For Catholics one of the greatest helps comes from the Sacrament of Penance. Teens know that one of the conditions for obtaining pardon is the resolution to avoid the sin in the future. They may and do forget that this includes the resolution to avoid the proximate occasions of sin. Parents can help teens greatly by reminding them of the obligation to avoid persons, places, or things which cause them to fall into sin.

Normally speaking, advice and warnings given in such a way as to win the voluntary co-operation of teens are almost a guarantee of victory in this teen-age problem. When advice and warnings fail, parents must stand on their authority in the matter of dates; but they must try to do it in such a way that it does not provoke teens to trample on their parental authority.

Teens are particularly touchy about criticism and regulation of their choice of companions. The reasons for this are many, but the fact remains. Juvenile delinquents are not the only ones whose parents are kept in ignorance of their companions. Many average teens conveniently forget to mention some of their companions, knowing full well that their parents would not approve. It is a somewhat natural attitude, not a malicious one; it is all part of a vague "don't fence me in" feeling.

Parents who are forced to forbid the continuance of certain companions have a special problem. The mere command to break off a friendship does not provide teens with the motive for obeying. They can find a hundred ways to deceive parents; and when they consider a command unreasonable they resort to all sorts of lies and deceptions. It is a sad day when a teen abandons his ideals of fair play to the animal standard of "don't get caught."

Until they have tried to get the voluntary cooperation of their teens to break up a sinful friendship, parents should not make use of their parental authority. But once they decide that such action is necessary, they must be prepared to be firm, and to use every means to enforce their command. The command itself should be accompanied by appeals to reason, the opinion of decent people, justice to the other party and to his parents, and the respect of their own children later on. This last point has more weight than people realize.

When the son of a mother I know returned from school one day he was so quiet that his mother became curious. She found him looking through some of the family papers.

"What are you looking for, dear?" she asked.

"I'm not one, am I?" he asked searchingly.

She looked over his shoulder. He was checking on the dates of his parents' marriage certificate.

Another serious fault of teen-age which should be discussed in this chapter is dishonesty.

Dishonesty in its various forms may be nothing more than another phase of teen-age; but if not checked it becomes a serious matter. The beginnings are innocent enough. They start in babyhood, are interrupted for a while, and are then renewed in teen-age.

As soon as a baby begins to recognize moving objects he has various bright-coloured toys dangled in front of his eyes. He learns early to reach for everything in sight, and forms a habit which has to be curbed when he is old enough to play with the toys of other children.

The tendency to want what we see does not

cease with the years. It grows stronger, even when the objects of our desires change. Our desire to want everything in sight fathers the advertising campaigns that run into millions of dollars each year. Teens feel the same attraction to material goods; and with the example of nations and so-called successful people before their eyes, some conclude they have a perfect right to take what they want. Once more the example of certain adults leads them to think that there is a difference of morality when they grow older.

This second or teen-age phase of dishonesty is more serious because it concerns not merely a chance impulse, but also will and intellect. But again, parents who understand teens know that fairness appeals to them more than cleverness. They need help to apply their own high standards to the practical things of life.

Fundamentally the teen standard of honesty comes close to the standard of the Commandment of God. The ingenuity of understanding parents must find the best way to help each individual teen to the realization of his own ideals. I remember quite an extreme case.

A mother and her teen-age son called on me one day, and in a few sentences explained that they had talked over his habit of stealing. As a result, they had decided to bring the problem to me. With this preparation she let us talk over the affair. We started talking class work, athletics, and school pals before we got down to work.

" How long have you been taking things that belong to others ? " I asked finally.

" When I was little I used to take things once in a while," he said, " but for the past two years I've been taking them all the time."

" Are they valuable ? " I asked.

" Sometimes yes, sometimes no," he said.

" Your mother seems quite generous and understanding," I said.

" I don't need anything," he said, " I just see stuff and take it."

" You are perfectly average in school," I said, " and in your studies a little above average. Except for this thing, you are as good as any lad in the school. Will you do something hard to break it ? "

" I don't know," he said. " What is it ? "

" First, you ought to receive the Sacraments at least once a week, to get God's help to make your will stronger. That's not the hard thing. Here it is. Every time you take anything you are to bring it to me or to your mother. We'll return it to the owner and try our best to keep you out of trouble. But if there's a penalty, you've got to pay it."

He agreed so quickly that I doubted his sincerity ; actually he never came to me with anything he stole. Years later we met again, and he brought up the incident himself.

" It was funny," he said, " but do you know,

I never had the desire to steal again. I don't think I ever will."

Repeating examples of this sort makes solutions sound very easy. Of course they are not. Habits are not acquired or overcome in a day. So parents need patience and courage to carry on, even when the results seem out of proportion to their efforts. *Building a man is not the work of days but of years.*

It is peculiar that many teens look on lies as necessary, and therefore somehow justifiable. Like so many adults, they probably consider lies the lesser of two evils. But it is peculiar that youngsters formulate a constant policy of deliberate lies and planned disobedience in their dealings with parents.

Often, as this book has tried to show, parents are at fault. Often enough they have not earned the confidence of their youngster, or have proved unfair in their manner of correction. But that's not the whole answer, and when a teen lies deliberately and without justification, strong measures are needed.

The lay headmaster of a small private school solved the problem of lying, in a boy who had me worried. Conditions at home, and the adult delinquency of his father, made his attendance at boarding school necessary.

During his pre-teen years disobedience covered by lies had worked very well. As a teen he regularly told his mother he was going one place when he was actually going somewhere else. He claimed to be with good companions when he was going with a crowd that was almost bad. During the last two years before he went away to school he went where he pleased, did as he pleased, and came home at night when he felt like it.

In spite of all that, I thought he could be a very normal youngster if given half a chance; and so helped make the arrangements for him to go away to school. The headmaster, let's call him Rod Smith, received all the authority of Teen's parents. Teen could not go out nights without the headmaster's permission, and the permission was to be given rarely. All letters were subject to Rod's censorship; and Teen agreed to try to do better.

During the first few months there was little real change in the boy except that he gave up his open defiance of authority. The difficulty of sneaking out nights in a small school kept him out of some mischief, and Rod practicing patience, tolerance, and forgiveness let Teen think he was getting away with it when he did sneak out. But Rod was shrewd and had a method in his silence; he was waiting for the right time to speak and act.

It came, as it always does. "One evening," he told us later, "Teen wrote a letter to a girl and submitted it for my approval. It was a nice letter and I told him so. But I was certain he showed me one letter, and mailed another."

"Pardon me a minute," Rod said to Teen, "there's something I want to see about. I'll be right back."

He got up quickly, leaving the youngster in his office. Sure enough, on Teen's desk was the other letter. He put it into his pocket and hurried back to the office. They talked for a few minutes more, then said good night. Teen was gone about half a hour, and then returned scared and white.

"I'm in trouble sir, "he said to Rod. "Can I talk to you?"

"Certainly," Rod said, as blandly as he could. "What is it?'

"I lost a letter tonight," he said. "I thought I left it on my desk. And if anyone finds it I'm in hot water."

"This one?" Rod asked, tossing it on the desk.

Teen didn't say a word, but just looked at him.

"You've lied to me constantly about various things," Rod said steadily, "and I treated you as if you were telling me the truth. You played me for a sucker. I let you get away with it because I thought you'd get wise to yourself. If you'd just be yourself you'd shoot square."

"What are you going to do, fire me?" Teen asked.

"Fire you!" Rod exclaimed, "fire you for

thinking I'm a dope? No, that's no reason for firing you. I'm going to punish you for trying to deceive me. And if you want to welsh on your agreement, you can quit."

Teen's head bowed. He picked up the unopened letter and tore it up. After a brief second's pause he looked up at Rod.

"What's the punishment, sir?" he asked.

PIETY

I LIKE Chesterton. "Christianity," said Chesterton, "has not been tried and found wanting. It has not been tried." If that's true, it cannot be called the fault of teens. For them to be religious is as natural as for them to be citizens of a country. They don't make their form of government nor their religion. In their developing years they accept these as they are handed to them. If teens find the form of government and religion good and practical, they give their loyalty with all the enthusiasm of youth; if they find their government or religion vague, more or less useless, or neglected, they have no time for them.

World War II provided us with excellent material for a study of Teen's religious habits. Called to the service of their country, teens had no gradual transition to adult life. Suddenly they were transferred from home to barracks, from peaceful living to efficient killings. They carried with them exactly what they received from their home influences. What they took was exactly what their parents gave them.

Monsignor Joseph F. Steadman before his death sent out a questionnaire to 700 military chaplains. Here are some excerpts from it.

"The Chaplains report," wrote Monsignor

Steadman, " that religious response of servicemen is better in combat zones and advance areas, but worse in United States and non-combat camps. Furthermore, men returned from the front become even more negligent. *Fox-hole religion* is reported as the religion of fear, too often unfortunately without the motive of love ; and so this type of religion ends when fear ends. Of course, it is only human to seek God when one is in danger or want, but the chief mainspring of New Testament religion is love, not fear ; its chief expression is adoration not petition . . . Hence, we may well ask ourselves, what has been lacking in our curriculum of teaching and practices ? "

" To myself I seem to be a realist seeing facts and reporting them," one Chaplain wrote, " not blinding my eyes with the example of a few men who are living saints. I am connected with a field that puts bomber crews through their final training before going into combat. In the past three weeks eight ships have crashed, 21 men have been killed, others badly hurt. I announce Mass for those killed, always a Catholic among them ; and maybe three or four attend Mass. It is a daily occurrence to talk to men who dropped the practice of religion when they donned the uniform. Confessions are few and ill-prepared. The way the men clear the chapel before Mass is over amazes the Protestants with its speed and efficiency. I have greater numbers at Mass than the Protestants although they far outnumber us. So what? Only about 30 per cent of the Catholic men here attend Mass on Sunday; about 18 per cent on Holy Days. And the Masses are at the most convenient times possible. With these facts is it honest to rhapsodize over the glowing faith and ardent charity of the men? If I am wrong tell me. I'd be glad to sing rather than to croak. Does all this make you feel like jumping in the air and shouting *Alleluia*? I've asked myself a thousand times, 'Why is it? What can I do?' My only answer is that the parents have failed, and there is not much you can do to counteract at least 18 years of indifferentism."

The chaplains reported that only about 40 per cent really and honestly practiced their faith; and of all the chaplains reporting, 56 per cent said that religion in the armed forces was just about the same in civilian life.

Teen's wartime qualifications cannot be called into question. His record as a fighter showed he could do hard things, that he was able to sacrifice his comfort, that he could give up life itself. To say that these same teens are religious cowards because religion is too hard is definitely unfair. The only logical conclusion is that religion as it has been presented to them, "18 years of indifferentism," has left them cold. And why not?

When Teen sees his dad wear a dinner suit on certain occasions, he knows it is merely for the show, and dubs it a monkey suit. When the same dad practices religion only on certain occasions, can Teen be censured for putting it in the same class with the monkey suit?

The marines of Joe Rosenthal's famous picture, who stormed Iwo Jima and raised the Stars and Stripes on Mt. Suribachi, did not think of themselves as pious, any more than they thought of donning monkey suits for the occasion. Yet they gave one of the greatest demonstrations of piety of the war.

If piety means folding hands and rolling eyes up to heaven, these men were not pious. But piety means loyalty to family, race, country, and God. Those youngsters on Mt. Suribachi gave definition of loyalty by their deeds. If many of them look on the word "pious" as synonymous with "sissy," if their religion is stored in moth balls with the monkey suit, the fault is not theirs but their parents'.

Religious teaching should come from parents. The Church, of course, assists parents by giving a more thorough explanation of doctrine, answering difficulties, and making practical application of doctrine to daily life. But the fact remains that parents should teach their children religion both by word and example. The function of State and Church is to assist parents in filling their obligations. *Only parents can have babies, and theirs is the first obligation in raising them.* All teens are interested in religion, just as they are interested in almost everything in life as it opens up before their maturing minds. Some teens come to regard religion as a burden, as something disagreeable. The fault is not theirs, but that of parents and teachers. Let's be honest and take the blame. We have let two faults creep into our teaching: too often we are impractical for a youngster's mind, and we have harped far too much on the negative side.

The first mistake concerns our manner of teaching. When teens think of home, or food, or a girl, or school, or religion, they think of it in reference to themselves. A beautiful doctrine, and a technical perfection in presenting doctrine, leaves them cold. *They will not be interested until they see how the doctrine has something to do with themselves.*

And negative teaching is even a more serious mistake. Who would not get fed up with religion if every practical application consisted of "thou shalt not!" Religion is essentially positive, life-giving, joyful. And if presented in the right way, the piety of religion makes a tremendous appeal to the hearts and minds of youth.

Because Jesus Christ is a Rebel, His ideals appeal to the heart of youth. He is the divine Rebel against the spirit of the world; and eventually each teen must choose between the freedom of Christ and the dictatorship of the world. Teens sense, even though vaguely, that they must avoid the traps of the passions, and that they want to see clearly just how to avoid getting caught by their passions. They want to know what they have to fight and how. Our job is to show them by example and instruction before they are enmeshed by the glamour and the false promises of the world.

During the war, our bomber crews were given more than general training. Before each mission they were briefed, and were given detailed information on how they were to use their knowledge against a particular objective. When the briefing was poorly done, as happened on some occasions, they dropped their bombs on their own men. The record seem to indicate that parents and teachers need to review their method of briefing teens.

And the father who stays away from church, or who makes little effort to be on time, is briefing his children to stay away from church, too, no matter what lectures he may give on the subject. The mother who comes from church only to be critical and uncharitable makes teens think that religion is like false teeth: to be used if things ever get that bad, but to be avoided if at all possible.

All parents know, though sometimes they overlook the fact, that healthy teens need a good deal of physical exercise, that they must have activity, and that interest in either play or work soon vanishes when activity declines. The same is true of religion. The explanation of doctrine and the answering of questions is not enough. Teen take an interest when they are called on to *do something* for their religion. Such activities need not all be directly religious. It is surprising what varied activities teens are capable of undertaking, and what sacrifices they can make.

A group of adults had interested themselves in work among the very poor children in the crowded section of the city. Their work was twofold: helping relieve some of the sting of poverty and teaching religion. But there were so many children that the adults could not take care of them properly, and they asked if I could get some youngsters to help.

The usual number volunteered. A day or so after my appeal a youngster stopped me in the hall; he was a tackle on the football team, and typical of what I suppose you'd call the rougher element of the school.

"Father," he said directly, "I don't know much about teaching, but I could show the kids how to box and play ball."

"Wonderful idea, Frank," I said. "These kids have a bit of a problem with discipline. Maybe you could help with that too."

He went to work at once. Soon he had organized the youngsters for games and was extremely popular. As some of the other lads had difficulty keeping discipline, he began attending their classes. It was enough for him just to sit there, and the class was strangely quiet.

I didn't know at the time that this boy himself needed help; and later on when I found out, I was very much embarrassed. He was a poor boy who cut his lunch down to get bus fare to the center; and when he finished his work with the youngsters he hitchhiked home. Of course he never said anything about it. I found out quite by chance.

Leadership, or at least some element of leadership, is latent in every youngster. Many people think that leadership is reserved for those who are endowed with certain personal qualifications which make them stand out from the crowd and act more or less alone. But that is false.

The majority of teens have some talent for leadership along particular lines. And religious organizations which provide group leadership appeal to them, for such organizations provide outlets for individual talents. And on the other side, teens, even the most aggressive of them, are conscious of their limitations. Group leadership in religious activities develops both their strong and their weaker abilities.

We must, parents and teachers, find more ways of attaining the active co-operation of youngsters in their religious training. While they rebel at dictatorship, they welcome co-operative effort.

A certain man told me that his reason for entering a certain profession was that it made it possible for him to leave home before he was of age without hurting the feelings of his parents.

And many a teen welcomed the last war because it got him away from home and school. True religion, lived in the home, strengthens the bonds between parents and teens.

Jesus Christ asked the Apostles to work with Him, not merely under Him. He established His Church and willed that all of its members should be coleaders with Him, assisting one another, each according to his own talents but always with Him. Parents and teachers are wasting their time if they try to change His plans or substitute some other method in place of His method.

YES OR NO

TEEN had just finished breakfast on a Saturday morning. He put his plate on the sink and started for the door.

"Teen," his mother called out with emphasis, "practice your piano first."

Teen started to mention certain plans for a game of ball; but before he could even start, his father's voice interrupted him.

"Wait a minute. Before you go out to play ball, you clean up the yard. And do a decent job of it this time!"

Morning is always the ideal time for family spats.

"Jim!" his mother said with more emphasis, "you know Teen must practice that piano. What are we paying good money for lessons for?"

"Well," said his dad, "the yard's got to be cleaned up. I'm not coming home every night to a junk yard."

Meantime, while Mom and Dad continued to argue about what job Teen should do first, sister Lulubelle came tripping down the stairs.

"Teen," she said sweetly but definitely, "run down to the post office and mail this letter for me."

Not because he wanted to, but because it provided a release from the argument, Teen went to mail the letter. When he got back the argument was still going, but somehow had moved up to a consideration of uncles and aunts on both sides of the family. Teen sat down to play with the dog, the only one in the house that seemed to like him as he was, or that seemed to think his ideas and plans were pretty good.

Actually it makes little difference on any given day whether music, or cleaning the yard, or the ball game comes first. A serious illness in the family, or anything else of importance, would be sufficient reason for letting all of them go. The strange thing is that Teen himself is not considered important. He is forgotten or at least taken for granted. Parents too often fail to reflect on the way their words and actions impress their growing teens.

"What's the matter?" I asked a teen who was wandering about listlessly. Ordinarily he was quite cheerful.

"Nothing," he said.

"You sick?" I asked.

"No."

"Something's wrong. Let's have it."

"Aw, my father and mother are fighting again."

Fighting changes a home into a house for discontented boarders; and no one can blame the teen-ager for being discontented in such an atmosphere. Consideration for their teens would prompt parents to practice and to teach by example the self-control which they expect their teens to learn.

Parental arguments are not the only situations in which teens are made to feel that they are pieces of animated furniture—to be shoved around or stuck in a corner according to the passing whims of their elders. Thousands of listeners are entertained each week by radio programs built around the confusions that result from lack of plan and unity in family life. The situations are humorous over the radio : the script is prepared that way. The responsibility for episodes is pretty evenly divided between various members of the family, and there is always a happy ending : the script is prepared that way too. In real life many tragedies arise from the same situations.

As I listened to a class of high school boys making preparations for a class picnic, the contrast between various homes was impressed on me very forcefully. The committee wanted to know definitely how many boys would go. There were three kinds of answers, and afterward I questioned them all to find out the reasons for the answers.

The first answer, from a few, was " No." Some had jobs and couldn't go. Some said their parents always refused permission for such forms of recreation.

The second answer was " Yes." Some said their parents always let them do as they pleased.

Others knew their parents would let them go, but would have to ask permission and tell them where they were going.

The third group said, " I have no idea if I can go or not." These boys were from homes in which plans were never definite for teens, and they just had no idea in the world what their parents' answer would be.

The last group was the largest. I gathered the impression that in the majority of homes parents give too little attention to a plan of play or work for teens.

A definite plan does not make teens like work any better ; most normal teens will escape work if they possibly can. Sometimes they are unreasonable about it. But a definite plan of work, play, and study trains them to a sense of responsibility ; and as a rule, a definite plan wins their voluntary co-operation.

While I was writing this chapter a daily paper published the results of a survey on this very subject. Some of the answers were very pointed.

" They (parents) wait until we want to play or go somewhere, and then give us some work to do."

" We recognize that we have to contribute our share of work in the home, but our parents ought to give us time for some of the things we like to do."

" Things used to be terrible at home. I was

always in the doghouse. But now we sit down, parents and children, and make our plans together, and there are no more arguments or meanness."

Definite plans do not have to be ironclad plans. In the same week I saw an example of a planned home, and one without plans of any kind. Yet the planned home was nothing terribly rigid.

We were sitting on the sun porch, three or four of us, when Teen came in to see his mother.

"Excuse me, Father," he said to me, and then turned to his mother. "Mom, can I go with some guys to play basketball?"

"Your work done?" she asked.

"Gee, by the time I finish all my work it'll be too dark to play."

"You didn't have much to do in the first place," his mother said. "You could have been out a half hour ago."

Teen turned away half-sullenly and started back to his job.

"You are the one who made the agreement," his mother said, "but it's a nice day. Go ahead, and finish your work tomorrow."

The boy finished the work quickly and in a cheerful mood. When he had gone, the mother explained that her boy was at the stage of teen-age when he would become listless and unreliable in spells. During such spells he responded to kindness, but became sullen under letter-perfect discipline.

The other mother was spoiling her son by excessive and unplanned kindness. Since her husband was dead, and the boy was her only child, her mistakes were quite understandable. She not only gave him everything and did everything for him ; but, worst of all, she let him do pretty much as he pleased.

The results of home environment were evident in school. Her boy was in my class in high school. He had good talent but expected to get marks without working for them. I couldn't raise the marks, so he sulked and complained to his mother. She was pretty bitter at first ; but after a few sessions in the parlour she began to admit that her darling was not perfect, and that her method of dealing with him might be improved. We worked out some sort of plan together, and I must say this for her—she really put it into effect.

Her lad pouted for weeks, and every time he looked at me he looked daggers. Of course I couldn't give him the satisfaction of knowing that I even recognized it, and after awhile he began to forget. Before the end of the semester he settled down to real study with his natural cheerful spirit. One day many months later I called him and told him to make a set of questions for a history quiz ; and after the test I had him correct the papers and grade them. He did a good job, but was much too severe in grading them. I regraded the papers and showed them to him. He laughed, half at himself, half at me.

" So all right," he said laughing, " Mary Magdalene became a saint too."

The ways in which teens want to be treated as important in the home are too many to discuss in detail. Parents should be glad that their teens are growing up, and should watch for opportunities to encourage them. If at the same time they are taught a sense of responsibility, and that a sense of responsibility is the true measure of their importance, there will be little danger of their abusing their new-found position.

Many parents seem to be unaware that their teens are growing up until they have to buy shoes or clothes some sizes larger ; and even then their attention is centered on the tape measure. But teens themselves are as conscious of their mental and spiritual advancement as their parents are of the price tag on the larger clothes.

Long before teens say " My parents treat me like a child," they have been thinking it ; and they are spokesmen for many other teens who lack the courage to put their thoughts and feelings into words. Of course no one would deny that the cry " My parents treat me like a child," is a demand for more liberty, more independence.

That in itself is a good sign. It is the sign that teens are drawing closer to the time when they must go on their own. And because they are approaching this very vital period of their life, they need more intensive and intelligent training. The spirit of independence must be moulded into self-reliance based on a sense of responsibility; and definite plans, definite time schedules for work, play, study, and social life do much to develop this sense of responsibility.

ON THEIR OWN

"BROTHERS DESCRIBE SLAYING OF MAN." With this headline a boy of fourteen and his brother of eleven made the front page of a metropolitan newspaper. When they were caught burglarizing a home, the older boy shot and killed the owner.

"Why didn't you tell your parents?" the eleven year-old was asked by police authorities.

"The lad looked wistfully at his sad-eyed stunned mother, sitting near by," reported the newspaper.

"I dunno," the youngster said slowly. "Mom and Pop were divorced."

When leaving the courtroom, the mother dropped a veil over her face to hide it from the photographers. "I cannot stand to have the world see my disgrace," she sobbed.

What did she mean? Just what was the disgrace? Did her son disgrace her by killing a man? Or did the killing make public the disgrace of her neglect and of her husband's neglect of the children?

Tragedies such as this prod civic and religious leaders into the realization that "something must be done." Many serious and many futile discussions result. Because the average teen is wholesome, the civic and religious leaders conclude that Teen is safe when under the supervision of home, school, or church. "But ah!" they say wisely, "leisure time is the danger time, because then Teen is on his own"!

This book isn't concerned with youngsters who have become juvenile delinquents, but with normal teens. The last statement—that the danger time is when a teen is on his own—is a platitude, and of course true. But not the first statement, that Teen is safe in his home. In a negative sense it can be true; but it may easily be false in the positive sense. The purpose of parental supervision is not merely to prevent Teen from robbing a bank while his parents look on: that is negative. The purpose of home training is to help Teen go straight when he's on his own: and that is positive.

And to help Teen go on his own, parents must have a few definite and fundamental rules as a guide; and they must help him to understand—not merely memorize—and apply these rules to actual teen situations.

Recently there was a teen-age craze in some places of stealing automobiles for an evening or until the gas tank was empty, and then abandoning them. Usually the machines were abandoned on some side street long before the police were notified of the theft. Many of the teens who did this were not in the juvenile delinquent class. They sought fun, excitement, and activity; and

" borrowing " machines for an evening suggested itself as quite a lark. Half the fun consisted in being able to steal the machine and abandon it without getting caught.

A teen-age girl told me in the course of a conversation that she used to climb out her window at night and join with other teens for joy rides. But the one thing she didn't like about the whole affair, she said, was the immorality that often took place during the course of the evening. She didn't like to drink, and wouldn't take on the petting, but she enjoyed every minute of the rides.

While the case may seem extreme, the confusion is something almost normal. She looked on impurity as something wrong, and had the courage to make her crowd respect her convictions. But taking the machines was not wrong to her mind, because there was no intention of keeping them. It was merely a matter of not getting caught. The minds of most teens have confusion about the applications of right and wrong. Had she been caught, her parents would probably have been " ashamed to have the world see their disgrace." Yet there was a failure some place—at home, school, or church—that made her unprepared to face life on her own.

Most teens know that there is a difference between breaking a law by parking a machine overtime and breaking a law by burglarizing a house. But when growing youngsters are confronted by the example of adults who take liberites with the law of God and man, there is little wonder at their confusion. It is little wonder that they will do some things that shock the sensibilities of human beings.

The human will must conform to the Divine Will and to the laws of society. So the duty of parents is clear : from week to week, as teens are faced with situations which they do not clearly understand, when teens meet difficulty in applying the Commandments of God or the state to daily life, parents must be ready to help them.

In many situations there will be conflict between the human will and the laws of God or the nation. The example all around them tells teens to ignore the law and do as they please if nice society approves or if they can get away with it. When there is such a conflict mere knowledge of what is right, especially confused knowledge, can't always stimulate the will to proper action. Teen needs the help of his parents whose words are an echo of the example they give.

This is not "theology" but "teenology." There are certain things a parent must teach slowly and patiently to a growing youngster. All of us want to get at the heart and mind of teens, see how good they are, and do our part to help them stay as good as God made them. It is not an easy job to raise a youngster, but it is a very rewarding job to raise him right.

Every teen must be taught the Commandments of God, not only the ones which concern the relation of the individual and his God, but also the ones which put definite obligations on us in dealing with our neighbour—respecting his right to life, to property, to a good name, and so forth. When teens know the Commandments of God well they know what is right; and that is why such knowledge is a fundamental rule for training them to go on their own.

And they must learn to respect the rights and feelings of others as sanctioned by civil law and by social customs. They must learn good manners.

Modern living has made it such a difficult lesson to learn; and teens are eternally confused by the confusion we have permitted of things *bad* in the moral sense and things *bad* in the opinion of society. It is no wonder when big nations, big business, big clubs, and big society arbitrarily arrange moral codes with less consideration than they give to the seating of official guests at a banquet table.

There are legitimate and highly necessary rights which custom gives to members of society to insure orderly and pleasant relations. These Teen must learn. And when custom dictates or permits anything contrary to moral rights or duties, he must learn how to assert his independence. Without help from older people, he has no way of knowing what "regard for others" demands of him; usually he is left to imitate his companions. One teen with personality and leadership is likely to set the pace for all the others.

This is not a question of good manners at table, weddings, dances, and funerals: common sense and rules of etiquette take care of such minor details. The problem is a different one, a deeper one. There is something inside a man which makes any rule mean one thing to one teen while it gives a radically different meaning to another. It is a question of the working out of individual personal character.

I remember two boys from the same family who were extreme opposites. The difference between teens of the same family is not normally so marked. Yet parents, to give proper guidance must be aware of the fact that no two personalities are the same. They must realize that each youngster needs individual treatment.

These two boys were as different in looks as in personality. The older one was dark, of medium height, heavy set, athletic; his younger brother was tall, fair, slender, of very ordinary athletic ability. The older was aggressive, the younger pleasant and reserved.

How could these two teens be expected to take the same meaning from the words, "Respect the rights of others," or "Stand up for your rights?" The younger one, popular with one set of boys because of his pleasant ways, needed the slogan "Stand up for your rights" to prevent his being led into trouble. His older brother, equally popular with a different set of boys, needed the slogan " Respect the rights of others " not because he was a bully, but because of his normal attitude toward authority or anything else that confined his liberty.

People who have a pessimistic attitude about modern youth usually feel perfectly safe in saying that the youngsters of today are too bold. Teens object to that. And the younger of these two brothers, and many teens like him, have a right to resent the unfairness of such a general condemnation. And if some of them try to live up to the reputation thus given them, it is difficult to blame them.

But the older brother? He and many teens like him may be called bold. He may be called rebellious against authority and against things which an older generation holds sacred. But he grows up in a world of adults who have made a religion of the natural human tendency to free ourselves from domination by others. As a nation, we are generous to a fault in giving, and we are stubborn to a fault in resisting any kind of force. If law-abiding citizens who surround a youngster make their own pet and private exceptions to law and customs, teens surely cannot be blamed for doing the same thing.

And teens see all this. They live in the midst of it. And if they acquire some of this " boldness," where do they get it? I maintain that adults of this type are bold, and that teens of this type are frank. And I love them for it, because I have found them always more willing than many adults to put principles before personal feelings after they learn the principles and after they learn how to deal with the inconsistencies of older people. Teens have not lived long enough to have a bad will. Their wills may be weak or misguided or undeveloped. But bad? No.

Teen-age is a miniature world whose citizens are neither children nor adults. Teens retain some of the characteristics of childhood while they are learning to be adults. And people who wish to help teens must show them which childhood characteristics to retain. It was Christ who said to adults, "Unless you become as little children you cannot enter the Kingdom of Heaven."

The good will of teens as a class is shown by their code of honour expressed with direct simplicity by the one word, *sportsmanship*. Adults who forget what that meant to them when they were teens cannot talk the language of teens. As a matter of fact customs and laws designed to protect the feelings and rights of others are, in reality, a detailed expression of what teens mean by sportsmanship. Sportsmanship is honest rivalry and graceful acceptance of results. It might make an important addition to national and international relations.

Lack of adult sportsmanship puzzles teens and does much to destroy their confidence in parents. I remember a teen telling me that he was recovering from an illness, and he wanted to go into the garden for awhile. The weather was somewhat cool, so his father refused the permission.

"There's too much danger of your getting a chill," the father said.

"But Dad, I'm good and warm," Teen answered.

"Your feet are cold right now," the dad said didactically.

"They're not ; honest, they're warm," Teen said.

"If your feet are cold," his father said, "will you take a licking ? "

"And if they're warm, will you ? " the youngster replied.

For the life of him, the teen-ager couldn't understand why his dad immediately became violently angry. And if the boy did have cold feet, he'd done nothing to deserve punishment. His question was asked as a part of a friendly conversation in which his father had made what Teen considered a sporting proposition. His father's immediate anger only increased the lack of understanding which had been growing between them.

Parents give intelligent help when they make use of qualities which Teen has, instead of trying to create artificial ones of the parents' own choosing. The most useful quality in teens is the one for which they are most condemned: *their determination to be independent.* When they are taught to assert their independence by choosing correctly between right and wrong leaders in morals, manners, and sportsmanship, they are taught to go out on their own.

With these lessons teens must be taught to cultivate adaptability, to exercise self-control. Teens are thoughtless; and thoughtless people are occupied with themselves or their own pet interests; they may or may not also be selfish. Adaptability is the trait which enables one to adjust his own interests to the interests of others. When and how to do that, and when not to do it, is quite a problem.

They may not adjust themselves into co-operation with moral evil; nor may they sacrifice a great good for harmony. Such a policy sows the seeds of hatred between individuals and the seeds of war between nations.

Normal adaptability concerns itself with small things. Even among adults most of the serious maladjustments have their beginnings in such trifling things as frowns, sharp words, and other superficial mannerisms. The feelings, once aroused, stimulate the imagination to erect spite fences.

Teens learn to get along with other teens through their own ideas of sportsmanship and normally from the demands of sportsmanship of their companions, often taught with small fists. Some do not learn the lesson, miss much of the joy of youth, and develop peculiarities of character. They need help, but hesitate to ask for it. Like everyone else, they have their talents as well as their limitations; parents can show them how to use talents to offset limitations.

At school badly adjusted teens rarely attract the attention of a busy teacher unless they make the odd mistakes for which they are noted. They tend to drift off by themselves; they feel alone; they brood. But they also give blind love and loyalty to anyone who treats them as normal teens. It would be a beautiful thing if the person who led them into normal living were always a parent.

ON THEIR OWN AT SCHOOL

"WHAT is the matter with that high school?" The father of two boys was speaking. His two sons and his friends' son were attending the same school.

"I don't know what you mean." said his friend.

"You've met my two sons," the father replied. "They are halfway through high school and are going to the dogs. They are a disgrace to me."

He went on to give details of all the mischief, some of it serious, that his boys were getting into; and of course in his mind the school was responsible. He didn't attempt to explain how the great majority of the boys at the school got along all right, and only his boys and a few others were in trouble.

His boys have our sympathy, as have all teens whose parents take little or no interest in them until they are in serious trouble. They are still average teens and can be saved, provided parents are willing to accept their responsibility and not blame others—least of all their teens—for their own parental neglect during pre-teen years.

The first year is the most important of all the high school years, for it is a test of what teens have learned as children, and is a laboratory which indicates what may be expected in the future. Freshmen in high school, regardless of their age in years, have graduated into the first phase of adult life.

To hear some people talk one would think that parents have done their duty when they have decided on a good high school for their teens; and that now they are free for work, social functions, and gin rummy. Do they really believe that a teacher with a class of thirty or forty students can take the place of a father and a mother for each individual teen?

Many parents have to make great sacrifices to send their teens to a good school. A good school is of the greatest importance not because it can take the place of parents, but *because it can better assist parents in the work which is properly theirs.*

This process of helping teens is not as complicated as some parents seem to think. Too often parents have no definite plan of action, probably because they are not quite sure what they are supposed to do. They make a good start by choosing the right high school, and hope that all will be well. Meantime they wait for something to happen to guide them to their next step.

Three months after school opened I spoke to the parents of a boy in the first year of high school. My purpose was to warn them in good time that their son had little chance of passing his midyear examinations unless he did better work. They were immediately solicitous.

"But what can we do?" they asked.

"See that he does his homework," I said. "He misses it frequently, sometimes copies it from other boys, and lies about it."

"Oh, is he doing that again?" they said.

They knew from his years in grammar school what might happen, but for three months they did nothing but keep their fingers crossed. When they found out that keeping their fingers crossed had no effect on their teen's conduct, they became very upset, and very indignant at him. But he had many good qualities, and I racked my brain to list every one of them.

They were stunned. They were almost as much upset by the recounting of his good qualities as they had been by his bad ones. Like so many parents, they did not realize that while learning to do things the right way, teens make unintentional as well as wilful mistakes.

And how can parents make up a program, instead of waiting for things to happen? How can they know what to do? It can all be put in one statement, even though there is grave danger of misinterpretation of the statement if some other meaning is given to it than the one insisted on throughout this book.

At the end of high school teens should know the importance of making the best of situations which they cannot change.

Though the statement has a bearing on academic knowledge and scholastic standing, that phase of it is not under consideration now. The words, "*situations which they cannot change,*" imply that there are many situations which they can change; and if these situations should be changed, teens should have some direction in what they call the "know how."

But the thing teens need to learn while they are teens is the thing that plagues the lives of many adults: how to deal with situations they *cannot change.* If they cannot adjust to unchanging facts and situations, they will feel at the very start of adult life like the soldier who had never worn a coat nor hat and was suddenly assigned to Alaska.

A teen in first year of high school meets new teachers and strange boys. He begins to form likes and dislikes for companions, teachers, and studies. He gathers a whole new set of impressions, some pleasant, some unpleasant. He is taking an adaptability test, though he is not aware of the fact, in how much he has learned during pre-teen years.

But parents are aware of the test, and must read his answers diligently and patiently in order to guide him. They can afford to take time for a work which is to be spread out over four years; and they must help him get a start on judging what things can and should be changed, and how to make the best of the ones that cannot be changed.

Another reason for taking time, and lots of time, with a youngster just starting high school is that neither Teen nor his parents knows exactly how much ability he has until he has tried to work out solutions of his own. Throughout his life he will have to go on his own. At this time of his life he needs a helping parental hand to show him how to correct his mistakes, to encourage him in spite of his failures, and to praise his efforts.

During the first week or two of high school, teens usually begin to tell their parents the things which reveal their responses to their new environment. They may come home bubbling with enthusiasm, or they may call the school a "dump." Those first impressions do not necessarily mean very much, for within the first six months they probably will be replaced by others.

But they are important to parents because they show how teens feel; and parents can quickly learn a teen's ability to cope with new situations. Teens who lack ability should not be allowed to keep going without help; and teens who ask for help should receive it. The surest way is to encourage a conversation about the difficulties encountered, to keep pushing a youngster to his own solutions; and then, when he is right, to give full approval to the way he has worked out his problem. Because it gives them confidence in themselves and prepares them to handle future problems, the best way to help teens is to *reason* to the right solution *with them.*

A youngster just starting high school comes home and calls the school a "dump." Perhaps he even wants to change to another school, any other school. In the course of a friendly conversation (and not a third degree) the only definite statement he can make is that he dislikes a certain teacher. He might easily be brought to admit that the subject taught by that teacher is the object of his dislike. Finally, he may be brought to see that the real trouble is that he dislikes any subject which he cannot grasp quickly and easily.

Now in all this there is something more important than the school, the teacher, the particular subject, or Teen's dislike for study. It is his ability to make the best of a situation, and to do it without running away from it. *The trait of avoiding hard things must be checked early, for it ruins many lives.* Once Teen knows and admits the cause of his trouble, half the battle has been won. But he will still need help.

The school can supply a coach for football, baseball, tennis, boxing, or swimming to do the work which parents cannot do. But teens need the home coaching staff in their personal lives. The student counselor and teachers can help; but no one can take the place of the two big coaches, Father and Mother.

Athletic coaches have an advantage over teachers for their pupils are already interested in their subject, and they have fewer persons to take their attention. Parents have the same advantage because teens are interested in themselves, and they like people who are interested in them.

Coaches have an advantage over parents in one thing: they study their pupils carefully to find talents and deficiencies. Because they have known their teens as children, parents often miss some talents, or some defects which become apparent only in teen-age.

Parents frequently miss the fact that teens consider themselves grown up; what is meant by the words *grown up* will depend on each teen. They may have a most childlike, and even childish, dependence on parents in some things; but they will be independent in others. Such behaviour would be inconsistent in an adult, but teens are not yet quite adults.

In one thing most teens become like adults very early: they resent anyone's attempting to pry into their mind and heart. The teen who talks freely with one he trusts goes on guard and resorts to lies if necessary as protection against the person who pries. Often enough that person is a parent.

Teens themselves may be at fault in this. Sensitiveness to what people think of them is an almost universal teen characteristic that makes them unduly suspicious of questions about themselves. Parents, through thoughtlessness, may give the impression that they are prying.

"*I am only trying to help you*" and "*I am doing this for your own good*" are trite sayings heard in almost every home. Parents are stating a fact, and hope thereby to win Teen's confidence. As a matter of fact, such statements have a meaning only when and to the extent that Teen's confidence has already been won.

The silent type of teen presents special problems. In a family of several children, the silent one stands out conspicuously, and often he is most inarticulate about himself. When reticence is natural to a teen he is not abnormal. He does not distrust his parents ; he is not even suspicious of them ; he has nothing that he is trying to hide. At times he may want to talk about himself. Generally the difficulty is that he does not know how.

Because it makes him all the more conscious of his difficulty, parents should never start by asking him direct questions about himself. The right way—not the easiest way by any means—is based on an *ability to listen to any subject he wants to discuss*. Then as a part of ordinary conversation, when Teen gets around to the personal angle, as he is bound to, parents can give the needed help.

Teens and adults have one problem in common : other people. Other people are a problem to us to the extent that we are a problem to ourselves, to the extent that we cannot be objective in our judgments. Parents can help teens to make the best of situations that deal with other people when they themselves are not involved in the conflict of personalities.

In theory we admit that other people have personal limitations proper to them as human beings; we even admit we have our own limitations as human beings. In practice when conflict arises we seem to expect the other person not to have, or at least to have overcome, the limitation which offends us.

Then when both sides are intolerant of the failings or limitations of others we have the conflicts of home, social life, business, and politics; and for teens, the conflicts of school.

We admire patience, tolerance, and forgiveness in others. When others are imposed on, we love them for being big enough to stand up under it. We want the friendship of such people. But for ourselves, we think we may be considered weak if we show generosity, tolerance, and forgiveness.

The teacher-teen clash of personalities is bound to appear many times in the course of four years of high school. For the most part Teen is responsible, though not always at fault. Thirty or forty teens with an oversupply of energy, and retaining the childhood inclination to play at the wrong time, can be very trying on any teacher.

Of course all is in fun until Teen gets caught. Then he gets "down" on the teacher, and perversely accuses the teacher of getting "down" on him. That, of course, is not peculiar to teens. Blaming the other fellow is typical of human nature. If there is nothing more than this to teacher-teen clashes, parents should make teens face the facts, and should make the adjustment in their own conduct.

But sometimes there is something more to it. All through life we must deal with the phenomenon of certain people being mutually antagonistic; no reason for the irritation need be apparent. With teacher-teens it has been immortalized in the line, "*I do not like thee, Dr. Fell; the reason why I cannot tell.*" Even the effort of one party to be friendly or kind irritates the other, and this antagonism may be present in greater or lesser degrees.

Such antagonisms can exist during teen-age. Teens cannot be expected to understand them without help, much less to know how to deal with them. They must be told the fact, and be persuaded to accept it without trying to place the blame for it. In this, as in all problems involving contact with other persons, feelings of bitterness and resentment blind us to actual facts, and lead us into actions which only increase misunderstandings.

"Adaptions to situations which cannot be changed" may mean that we must avoid forcing our friendship or even our company on certain people, but at the same time be ready to receive and return signs of friendship from them. *Indifference towards a person that comes from the acknowledgment of his right to pick his own friends is vastly different from the snubbing that is born of hurt feelings.*

For the most part teen problems in dealings with teachers and others in authority are the result of Teen's own thoughtless actions, and sometimes of his deliberate ones. To convince him of that takes time. Parents have four high school years during which they can give Teen a good start in learning how to deal with other people.

But each youngster will need a different sort of schooling to learn to accept the responsibility for his actions. Parents must determine what sort of training their own Teen requires; then they must be ready to make use of the many opportunities which Teen will provide.

FROM DIAPERS TO DATES

THE changes that take place between childhood and teen-age are great ; but they are so natural that they require little thought, and are so gradual that they attract little notice from parents. And all during this period of teen growth parents tend to become more set in their ways, and less likely to adapt their thinking and planning to the changing outlook of their children.

Teen's first year in high school is the logical and the psychological time for parents to revise their dealings with Teen, and to guide them into more mature lines.

From first high on, if it hasn't been done before, parents must give particular attention to family conversations with their children. Teens gather impressions and form habits of thought from the constant attitude of their parents in ordinary conversations.

Children are told to keep quiet when older people are speaking.

Children are told to leave the room during some conversations.

Children are listened to with indulgent smiles.

Children often provide humour when they express their own ideas.

Children often get a halfhearted " Yes " or

"No" to their remarks. Translated it means, "*I know you are in the room with me, but I certainly wish you were out playing in the yard.*"

But there are no children in high school; and parents ought to recognize this fact from the very first day of school. A change in the manner of dealing with teens tells them that their parents respect their years. No one should smile at that statement when thinking of their own pudgy youngster. Parents of high school youngsters should never treat Teen as a child—unless they want him to transfer his confidence to someone outside the home.

In the world of adults we concede to others the right to express their opinions, no matter how much we disagree with their views. Teens granted the same right reveal their trends of thought. They are pleased when their parents approve, and are willing to listen when parents attempt to show them how they may be wrong.

During these family conversations, usually started by teens themselves, parents can make use of the opportunities provided to help build character. They can use the conversations to direct ambitions of youngsters into lines in keeping with their talents.

All teens want to be good at something; too often the difficulty is that they do not know what. I saw a little boy come out of a western movie, stand behind a telephone pole, and shoot from the hip with a toy gun at passing automobiles.

His imaginary world was so real that he was unconscious of the smiles of adults passing by.

Teens (and adults too) can and often do live in a world just as impractical, though less imaginary. Their efforts to be good at something, to be outstanding, sometimes end in failure and discouragement. That could easily happen to a youngster in the boxing ring if the coach failed to teach him his proper weight and class. A featherweight may read *Superman* in the funnies, but he does not feel disgraced when he can't knock out a heavyweight.

Actually a boxing coach does more than tell teens what class they are in and then hand them a pair of gloves. He gives them exercises according to a definite plan; the purpose of the plan is to show teens how to take care of themselves. He spends time giving them confidence in themselves and enthusiasm for the hard grind of training.

Realization of any ambition in life demands that we do things hard and disagreeable. *And teens, contrary to any other opinion, are not afraid of hard things provided what is demanded is not beyond the limits of their talents and disposition of character, and provided they see a good reason for the sacrifice.*

Frequently, as adults know from experience, the good results of effort are not apparent at once, though difficulties and disagreeable elements are very evident. In these cases, the motive for doing hard things must be made clear to teens; the best motivation comes through showing them that the results of their effort will be the realization of one of their own ideals.

Youth seeks action; and youth has high ideals though he does not understand them clearly. Given the proper guidance, youth tries to realize his ideals in action. Teens do not even know that their ideals are particularly high. They do not know how good and lovable God made them. They just try to be themselves in a world of contradictions. Even the dead-end kid who hates a cop is loyal to the gang, and is living up to an ideal.

One evening the parents of a teen girl asked over the phone that one of the Fathers please come and straighten out a home problem which was beyond them. When he arrived the girl was ready to go out with a crowd of jitterbugs in defiance of parental orders. When he spoke to her she refused flatly to do the bidding of her parents.

"My relatives were given to me," she said bitterly. "Thank God, I can pick my own friends."

In a spirit of reckless anger she poured out all her pent-up rebellion against home, parents, and everything connected with them. No doubt she expected the Father to be shocked or indignant. Instead, without approving of anything she said, he encouraged her by questioning to get the whole thing out. You can give an understanding and sympathetic hearing without condoning disrespect for authority.

Gradually she became more calm, more willing to reason things out. The Fourth Commandment as it applied even in her case provided the motive for submission. She actually wanted to go out, not so much to be with friends as to be away from home. She stayed home that night through a sense of duty, not through any feelings of love for her parents.

But she had a capacity for loyalty to duty as well as to persons. At home that trait was not recognized by her parents. They saw her faults, and they told her about them. With all their good intentions they drove their daughter to think, "*Thank God, I can choose my friends.*" That was compensation: she was looking for an object for her loyalty.

A compensation is anything good, bad, or indifferent which Teen substitutes for something better that he has failed to do. Society shakes its head over the juvenile delinquent who uses his gift of leadership to boss a gang of teen-age thieves. Society should use its own head to direct the energy and enthusiasm of that youngster into better channels.

During the Christmas holidays a teen asked his parents for permission to quit school and go to work. He expected failures for the midterm examinations, and could not see how he might possibly pass at the end of the year. When he met refusal, he proposed that he drop the regular high school course and take up manual arts.

The facts of his high school career were interesting. When he started he worked hard—at football. Studies he kept up just enough to remain on the squad. But he wasn't a good enough football player, and failed to make the squad. Naturally disappointed, he began to brood, and lost all interest in study. He caused no trouble and attended class regularly; but his was the mechanical regularity of a department store escalator.

Training in manual arts is a good thing; for some teens it may be the only thing. For this teen it was harmful. He was running away from a difficulty instead of facing it. He was seeking compensation. Very often teens seek this compensation in the companionship of other teens. Water seeks its own level, and the problem of companionship is always a thorny one for a person who is dealing with teen-agers.

Teens need guidance in choosing their companions; but there is no problem on which they are less willing to accept help. None of us can account for our likes and dislikes of persons, and of course it takes much more than goodness or the approval of parents to make for companionship. Counseling teens on companionship is made difficult by the fact that none of us may want to accept without proof that an enjoyable companionship may also be harmful or bad.

In the course of some work I was doing I met a girl, an independent little spitfire, who with disarming frankness was the first to admit that she was an independent spitfire. She came to see me fairly often and brought a companion just as independent, but a bit less fiery. They realized they were drifting away from their own ideals and asked for some help. One time at school they got into trouble that threatened to become quite serious. I listened for some time to her recital which cascaded out like a swollen stream.

"There's no difficulty about it," I managed to say at last. "Your pal is bad for you. You know that most of your troubles start when you two get together."

She heard only the first four words, "Your pal is bad . . . ." All her loyalty, that grand but too little appreciated virtue of teens, surged up in fiery defense of her girl friend. It was some time before I got a chance to speak again.

"Let's put it this way then," I said. "You're bad for her!"

"Well, that's different," she said.

"I know you; you've told me about yourself," I said slowly. "I know her too; she's told me of herself. You are both good, but you are not good for one another." It took a lot more talking on just this point to make it clear, but eventually it did become evident.

"Should old acquaintance be forgot," she

said, and smiled wryly as she left. "Maybe once in a life time isn't too much. Thanks."

In this affair both teens were good; both had an independent spirit beyond the average; both had been provoked to rebellion by their parents' abuse of authority. When they met at school and found that they had similar experiences, and that they felt the same way about their experiences, they had a bond of friendship. Each one encouraged the other in her independence and disrespect for authority. No longer were they helping each other to make the best of a bad situation. Now they were helping each other make a bad situation worse. They had to understand that before they could see that they were bad company for each other.

They would have ignored me had I tried to choose their companions for them. They were average teens, and average teens like to pick their own companions. Even if they had conceded, out of respect for me, they would have obtained but a solution to an individual problem, and they would have missed preparation for a time when they would have to choose companions without advice.

When parents realize that certain companions are bad for their own youngsters they must proceed with caution. The idea must be sold, and not rammed down a teen throat. It would be a difficult job to persuade an adult of the same idea. Long before the subject was brought up, there would be conferences, plans, suggestions—many of them considered and rejected before a final approach was selected. To persuade Teen of the same fact is not easier ; it is infinitely more difficult. And yet he responds well if the idea is wisely presented.

One afternoon after school a woebegone teen passed me in the corridor. A more forlorn youngster I'd never seen.

" Pull up your chin," I said to him, " or you're going to trip over it."

He stopped, looked up at me with respectful deadness, and didn't say a word.

" No game ? " I asked.

" I gotta go to study hall," he said.

" More trouble," I said calmly.

" Yeah. I mean yes, Father."

" You're not much trouble in my class," I said.

" How come all this ? "

" I don't know," he said.

There was a ream of conversation in a similar vein. My own voice was trying its best to sound sympathetic, and his answers were in monosyllabic grunts.

" Isn't it true," I said finally, " you rarely get into trouble except when you are with a certain bunch of fellows ! "

His manner changed quite a bit. " Father," he said, and there was appeal in his voice, " we have an awful good time together."

"But with them you're always in the dog-house," I said.

"We don't intend to get into trouble; but when somebody starts something we all get into it," he said.

"Well, don't you have any influence on them?' I asked.

He thought it over for a minute. "You mean I ought to tell them what to do?" he asked.

"Why not!" I said. "Aren't you as much of the crowd as anyone else?"

"They wouldn't pay any attention to me," he said with finality.

"Add it up, pal," I said bluntly. "According to your own words, you're not one of them. They let you hang on, and get into trouble, and take the punishment—all for the privilege of doing what they tell you. Why don't you be smart and pull out?"

"I'll be seeing you," I said, and walked away. As I turned the corner, I stole a look at him. He was still rooted in the same spot, staring thoughtfully at my retreating back.

No problem of companionship requires more delicacy, finesse, and salesmanship than that of "dates" and going "steady." Because they fear that such an admission encourages their parents to impose unreasonable restriction on them, teens are almost always reluctant to admit the dangers involved.

I asked three rather outstanding teens for help in finding a solution; they came to their conclusions entirely independent of one another, in response to the same questions. All three freely admitted the need of parental supervision of dates.

The first one said that good parents by being too strict as teens grow older force teens into lies and deception, and prepare them to be reckless on their nights out.

The second teen tried to work out a graded program for the different years of high school. Younger teens would have to be home at an earlier hour and would be allowed out less often; as they increased in age, so would they increase in privileges. The program had the advantage of being very definite.

"But," I said, "do you think teens would submit to it?"

He shook his head. "I'm afraid not," he said with a shy smile.

The third teen went through the same process of reasoning, arrived at the same conclusions, and rejected them all.

"There is only one solution," he said finally and without any prompting from me. "Parents must have the confidence and trust of their children."

No one can add anything to that.

TEEN AND STUDY

SOME teens, so they tell me, really like to study. The majority of teens, with the help of their teachers and parents, can eventually learn to take an interest in studies. Depending on their talents, their grades range from poor to satisfactory, and from satisfactory to excellent.

The ones who range from failure to satisfactory are the ones who really need guidance and encouragement. And they are the ones least likely to get it. Ordinary mischief, normal in teens, overlooked in the brighter luminaries, brings a harsh reprimand and punishment to the more backward. Home and school both take on the aspect of torture chambers, and teens seek escape from both.

There are exceptions. I remember one freckled redhead who showed a genial resignation, and a judgment remarkable for a lad in first year high. His first semester was pretty much of a failure, but it didn't dim his cheerful grin, nor keep him from trying to do better.

In the second semester he and a few others were put into a special class, the class for dumbbells he called it. After a few weeks I met him and asked how he was making out.

"I hope I'll pass all right," he said. "If I can get through in these other subjects, I'll go in for science. Math comes easy to me. Some of the fellows are as dumb in math as I am in other subjects. I know just how they feel."

He'd faced his limitations without discouragement, and had recognized his talents; he'd even planned a future based on his talents. This lad had figured the whole thing out himself. But the average teen cannot be expected to do so without help.

Parents must give this help; but they must cautiously avoid any approach that resembles the approach of pre-teen years. To tell teens what is best for them, and then to expect them to act immediately just on the authority of parents is proper to *pre-teen* years. With *teens, parents must arrive at conclusions through logical discussion and sympathetic understanding*. Such a course has the further advantage of helping train them to go on their own intelligently.

At intervals throughout the year all teens get tired of the regular grind of the classroom and of study. Like a stout person on a diet, they find that knowing what is best does not always mean doing what is best. Sometimes punishment, or the threat of punishment, may have to be invoked. *But punishment should be the last resort of parents who want to train their teens to meet life well.*

There is a way to advance Teen's interest in study. Parents must become interested in his studies, not just generally, but moving with him from day to day. Teens pay a compliment to their parents when they ask for help in studies. The request for help implies confidence in the willingness of parents to help, and is a tacit admission that Father and Mother know more than they do.

I remember quite well two lads in my class and their dads. The father of the one had a fair education; but work and the circumstances of life had kept him out of contact with book knowledge until his son started high school. At first he was able to give the help his son asked, but before very long he found himself unable to work out the problems. He freely admitted his inability to help; and he asked his son to get the answers from the teacher, and to explain them to him at night. He didn't know that he was using the best possible psychology to stimulate the interest of his teen; he was just being honest and interested. But the effect on Teen was better than almost anything else he might have done.

The other dad, a lawyer, was exactly the opposite; he was not only very well educated, but studious by nature and very well read. He could give the right answers on almost every subject in high school, and he gave them—briefly, quickly, and with a certain amount of impatience. The youngster mumbled, "Yes, yes, yes," to all the explanations; but back at school the next morning he gave a poor account of himself. Very soon he stopped asking questions, and the father was always a disappointed man because the son never rose higher than mediocrity in his school years.

Too often, parents who feel " rusty " on schoolwork think they are disgraced because they have forgotten so much. But not at all. Not the best teacher in the world is able to remember offhand everything he has learned. Teens see through bluff or pretence quickly, and they don't ask encyclopaedic knowledge from parents. They would like *interest.*

Because of their constant association with books, teachers are expected to have more book knowledge than parents. The fair-mindedness of teens makes them accept that fact. But when parents lose interest as the subject becomes difficult, teens are inclined to so the same. *One of the best ways for parents to draw tighter the bond of love between themselves and their teens is to work out hard problems with them.* Even total strangers become friends when they have the same problem and need one another's help in working out the solution.

All teens find some subjects harder than others. They generally find difficulty with a new subject, for they don't quite understand what they are supposed to do, nor how to go about doing it. Like all the rest of us, they tend to have more interest in the studies that come easy to them; and they build up a dislike for the ones they find difficult.

By helping teens with their difficulties in studies, parents do more than help them with a temporary problem. All too soon the swift years bring the obligations of parenthood; and the meaning of *home* cannot be learned in a classroom, but only in a home.

I once listened in on a conversation between a teen girl and a father famous for his influence with teen-age youngsters.

"You never condemn us, not even the bad ones," said the teen.

"I'm an old man," the father said, "and the years have taught me that even when they do bad things, teens themselves are only slightly to blame. I have to condemn the bad things, but I've learned not to condemn the teens."

"What about the parents of such teens? Should they be condemned for the things their children do?" I asked.

The teen-ager's eyes flashed. "Of course they should. They're responsible, aren't they?"

"Are they?" the father asked.

"Don't you think so?" she asked hesitantly.

"Parents need as much understanding as their delinquent teens," he said. "Some are selfish individuals who have broken their homes by infidelity or divorce. But I think there are many parents of delinquents who *never had a good home when they were teens*. They didn't learn much from their own parents, so they don't know how to think with, and to win the confidence of their children."

"It must be awful not to know how to talk to your own children," she said. "But, father, how did you ever happen to think of it?"

"From the teachings of our Lord," said the father, "and from His example. He condemned many bad deeds, but few persons. He understood people, so He forgave and instructed them."

His simple expression of a profound truth made a deep impression on me. All parents know that the majority of teens will eventually get married; and all parents have a vague feeling they should give some training for parenthood. It is a vague feeling that there should be something in it more than an instruction about sex.

And of course that vague feeling is a right one: the glorious vocation of parenthood is the physical, religious, and intellectual training of youth, the building of men and women for God and country, the creation of homes for the future.

The example of parents, their habits of thinking and acting, the spirit that dominates the family—from these come Teen's training in parenthood. Sometimes it is good training, sometimes it is bad. But at all times it is the major source of Teen's ideas about home.

This chapter on "study" would be only half written if it neglected to mention the education of teens in the dignity of labour. The emphasis placed on white-collar jobs is not only exaggerated but harmful. Very many teens are certain to find their livelihood in the large and lucrative fields of manual labour. This is no disgrace, nor should it be a handicap.

Recently a group of men formed a discussion group to prepare speakers on the labour question. There was only one condition for membership, interest in the subject. The club was composed of professional men, mechanics, and labourers. Eventually they fused into a smooth-working organization. But in the beginning some of the men felt out of place.

"After all, I'm only a labouring man," one of them said.

The man who feels that somehow he is inferior just because he is a labouring man is, through no fault of his own, the victim of a spirit which is neither Christian nor American. As long as he continues to feel that way he is an easy victim of an unscrupulous employer or of an equally unscrupulous labour leader.

American teens must be given an understanding of the dignity of labour and an education which will prepare them to be articulate in forming the policies of labour unions. Then they will have a better chance to raise working and living standards to a level worthy of their dignity.

The professional man and the white-collar man must be as interested in this as is the working man. It is a major part of good citizenship.

ATHLETICS

SO much has been written about athletics that mention of the subject here may seem superfluous. But truths which we know and facts which have been verified are easily forgotten. So, a reminder of the importance of organized athletics in the lives of teens may not be out of place.

All intelligent educators know the effect athletics have on the physical growth, development, and well-being of youth. They welcome the training that comes from co-ordination of brain, eye, and muscle, the character building that comes from discipline, and the social and moral strengthening that comes from teamwork.

Teen needs athletic competition (even if he never makes a team) for all those reasons; but some might forget that one of the most important reasons for athletics is the unadulterated fun, the carefree, healthy, absorbing enjoyment that teens get from physical play. That is part of normal teen life. And it is part of normal parenthood for parents to be interested in and to share these joys with their teens.

Very often the attitude of parents toward athletics is the crossroad which decides whether parents and teens travel together or go separate ways.

I know a dad who was obsessed with the idea that rigid discipline was the essential thing in raising his boy. He constantly harped on study, work, serious-mindedness; this, he thought, was the only way to offset his son's inclination to play. Only very seldom, and as the result of long pleading, would he relax to give the boy permission to take part in some game or sport which should have been a regular part of the teen's life.

"Partly because I loved him and partly because I was afraid of him," said the young man, "I submitted to dad's ideas for a long time. But by the time I was fourteen rebellion had pretty well taken the place of love. I found ways of going out with my gang, and my dad rarely caught me. Even when he did catch me I was too good a liar for him to discover all the things I did. A deep love and respect for my mother was the only thing that kept me from going completely bad."

The father of this boy must have been deprived of the normal joys of boyhood. Had he experienced the comradeship that grows between parents and their teens through mutual interest in sports, he would not so soon have become an old man with nothing in common with his own teen.

But what about his contention that teens are inclined to take too much interest in play? Isn't it true that this interest is the cause of neglect of study and of other duties?

Certainly it is true in most cases. It is a sure sign that teens are normal, just as they were normal children when they preferred candy to cereal, and ice cream to vegetables. Naturally most teens go to extremes in sports when given the chance. Few of them without guidance know how to keep a balance between duty and pleasure.

But the implication that parents who take an interest in athletics make the situation worse is simply untrue. On the contrary, parents who do not take an interest are the ones whose guidance makes no impression.

"My parents live in another generation," teens say.

"My parents don't want me to have any fun," they say.

"Gee, my parents are old," they say sadly.

Teens cannot say that about parents who live in the present with their teens. Consequently teens with such parents give more attention to explanation, admonitions, and punishment when these prove necessary.

In keeping a balance between duty and pleasure, the guidance of teens requires the three steps of explanation, admonition, and punishment; and they should be taken in that order, so that punishment is used as a last resort.

I had a youngster in freshman college whose talent was ordinary, but whose interest in study was excellent. But after a fine start he grew increasingly careless in studies. A conflict between football and study was the cause of the trouble. That, at least, was what I thought, though I didn't mention it to him.

One morning, about the middle of football season, he reported that he had done nothing on an assignment due that day. It had happened before, but this day he wanted to give a justification. He said that after intensive football practice he found it impossible to accomplish anything in study. He'd tried putting in long hours at night, but his mind was so dull that he could make no progress.

"I suppose the only thing is to give up football," he said. It was half question, half statement.

But that was not the answer. He was a good player, an important cog on the team, a great contributor to the spirit of the school. He had some free time during the day, and some of it could reasonably be applied to study. Some work might have to be neglected, but it would have to be made up after the football season. He finally made out a schedule for himself and followed it, and he had a successful year both in studies and in athletics.

Teens are wonderfully co-operative when approached in the right way. Parents can find a hundred different ways of getting the desired results before they make use of punishment. Yet parents must be patient, and they must be tolerant. Teens will need many reminders and many explanations.

Most of the disappointment and impatience that parents experience in dealing with their teens comes from failure to realize that thoughtlessness is normal in youngsters. Their enjoyment in play is so complete that they think of nothing else. That's not an excuse: it is merely an explanation that thoughtlessness, far more than bad will, makes teens slow in learning how to keep a balance between duty and pleasure.

But there are teens for whom a lack of interest in athletics is perfectly normal. They may be artificially stimulated to take some interest in sports; but such interest is not the real thing and does not last long. Actually, it is just as impossible for them to learn to play a game well as for some people to learn to drive an automobile well. It is not easy for a person normally interested in sports to learn that some people simply have no such interest—have no interest actually in *watching* others play. It was a lesson I found very difficult to learn; and before I learned it I made mistakes which still cause me great sorrow.

These teens have, or should have, other interests which are play for them. That their interests are usually of a more serious nature makes little difference. The main danger is that physical exercise, so important for youth, can be neglected. Merely to tell this type of teen that exercise is necessary for health makes little impression. The best results are obtained by encouraging a hobby which requires physical effort. Just how much teens can be expected to do in any line—study, work, or play—depends entirely on how much their interest has been aroused.

SANCTIONS

A TEEN-AGE boy had just been punished by his father. A few minutes later he was outside the house, where his mother heard a friend sympathizing with him.

"Oh, dad means well. He just can't help himself," said her youngster with resignation.

Teen knew that the punishment indicated his father's mood rather than his own fault; and being of a more even temper than most teens, he tried to ignore the whole affair.

The purpose of sanctions is to train teens in the self-control necessary for right conduct. Punishment by whim, mood, or feeling is an exhibition of lack of control in parents. No wonder teens become indifferent, and even rebellious, against that kind of discipline.

The whole idea of a sanction is to apply force when necessary to make sure that teen will learn the right thing for the time when he will be independent of parental control. Keeping that purpose in mind, good parents follow certain steps to enforce discipline.

The first step is an *explanation* of the fault noted, with an explanation of why it should not be repeated.

The second step is an *admonition*. Everyone forgets.

The third is the *alternative*. It is a definite order to which a definite penalty is attached; its purpose is to give Teen his free choice.

Then comes the *deluge*. The penalty should be made, as far as possible, proportionate to the fault. It should be in the same matter in which the fault is committed. And once assigned, a just penalty must be enforced. And it is extremely important that both parents agree so that one parent never vetoes a penalty assigned by the other parent.

What shall we do with the high school football hero who suddenly decides that lessons are merely for those greasy grinds who sit in the stands? His parents want him to do better in studies. And being wise, they do not want to deprive him of football. Their purpose is to lead him, not force him, to strike a balance. First come explanations which fall on ears made deaf by touchdown applause. It is time for an admonition, a warning that unless he does better in studies restrictions will be made on football. Its general purpose is to stimulate Teen to voluntary amendment.

How often during the years I've gone through this conversation.

"My father see you yet?" the teen-ager asks with some trepidation. "How am I doing in my studies?"

Generally there is some slight improvement, and I tell him so.

"Will you write a note to my dad and tell him that?"

"Why?"

"If I don't get better marks, I'm going to lose out on football. Or if it isn't that, it'll be something just as bad."

Often admonition fails to get satisfactory results. Then the time for the third step, the alternative, has arrived. He is told definitely what he is expected to do, and definitely what to expect if he fails. Explanations and admonitions should be repeated often enough and clearly enough that Teen knows the particular subjects in which his work is not satisfactory. And he must be made to understand that excessive interest in play is the cause of his failures. Of course admonition implies penalty, definite penalty.

A penalty always requires thought. It must be proportionate to the fault, and wherever possible in the same matter as the fault. Parents should talk over a penalty with great consideration. It must be possible, it must be just, and it must be enforced if such a step becomes necessary.

Teen is doing badly in history; there is a good deal of homework which interferes with his football practice or social desires associated with football. The penalty should not be to give up football for the rest of the season. But it should deal with some other form of play, movies, dances, parties, nights out, the school prom, his use of the radio or 'phone—perhaps the thing next to football most precious to him.

Just as Teen should know definitely what is expected of him and should know the penalty for failure, so also he should understand clearly that he is making a choice between one and the other. Should he, in fact, choose the penalty, he gives notice that the penalty was not severe enough; next time it should be more severe, and he should be told why. By keeping him in the position of making definite choices and taking the consequences, parents build up Teen's sense of responsibility.

But he shouldn't ever be threatened with a punishment that is unjust or too severe. Such a thing happens when parents determine the penalty under the influence of whim, mood, or feeling. Then they are placed in the dilemma of harming Teen whether they enforce or dismiss the penalty.

A parent in the home, like the teacher in school, needs steady nerves, almost infinite patience, and a sense of humour to cope with all of the smaller matters of discipline. None of them is important in itself; yet the sum total does much to form the character of Teen. There are the plaguing little problems of neatness and good manners, noise, moodiness, and the so-called laziness of growing teens. None of these is serious by itself, and it should not receive the same treatment as a more serious fault.

The mother of a boy called at school and asked me to use my influence on her teen to make him behave better at home. Eventually I was using what influence I had to make her behave better. Her whole method was faulty.

"John," she invariably said, "the next time you do that I'll punish you."

Of course, like any normal teen, he did it again.

"John," she said, "the next time you do that I'll punish you ! And I mean it."

After he had done the same thing time and time again, she would become exasperated and punish him severely. It caused him to feel disappointed that he had not figured her mood more correctly.

"She practically never means what she says," her lad told me.

In another home where there were pre-teens and teen-agers, the children were noted for their good manners and generally excellent training. I was at their home one time, and told the parents of the nice things I'd heard from different sources about their children. I asked them about their system of training.

Of course they were pleased that somebody should see some results from their efforts. The, slow progress and many failures of their children, the long daily grind of trying to be good parents was discouraging. They had worked out a system of their own, although they were honest with themselves in admitting their own mistakes.

As we were talking one teen was reading, one was washing dishes, and the others were playing. The mother explained that there were certain set penalties for repeated faults, and all the children knew what they were. The teen who was washing dishes alone was paying for his failure to dry them well the night before when it was his turn to help with the dishes.

I asked her about some of the other penalties. Before answering, she explained that often she found it better to pretend not to see some of the failures. She gave as example a rainy day when the weather prevents young people from expending surplus energy: on such days anything can happen.

Most of the penalties grew out of the circumstances of the home. At one time the children had complained of unfairness in assignment of tasks. She overcame that by rotating them among all of the jobs, and for the most part working them in pairs. But they promptly thought up more problems.

They wasted time in their work, and stretched half-hour jobs well over an hour, and then complained about the amount of work they had to do. The mother had playtime follow work, so that what time was wasted came out of playtime. In the evening, when that was not practical, fooling over the dishes meant missing a favoured radio program.

To think that this settled the matter of discipline is a slander on the ingenuity of youth. Nothing in this chapter settles any problem of discipline. Nothing here is presented as an unfailing chart. Rather, the direction which discipline should take is indicated. You are not at fault when you break rules of the sort given here, unless you break them unknowingly.

The mother soon found that the one who had incurred a penalty would by various means interfere with the others ; misery loves company. The problem was further complicated by counterclaims in which each one accused the other of starting the trouble, until all sounded like a general meeting of the United Nations. But the mother kept eyes and ears alert, so as to have some facts from personal observation. Often there was enough fault on both sides to justify a common penalty.

One of the most effective penalties was the loss of special merits and rewards. The rewards were intended to develop a sense of responsibility in the youngsters. The test of responsibility was the ability to do the chores assigned without prodding. The greatest reward was graduation from certain jobs they disliked. But every time they lost special merits they delayed the time of their graduation. It took a long time to graduate, and she kept providing her "school" with new pupils.

It is almost impossible to estimate the harm done when parents disagree on punishments. In fact they should never discuss the subject of punishment in the presence of their children until they know that they agree. The modern teen reacts quickly to indecision in this matter.

"Well, pals, make up your minds," he says to himself.

And when the final decision is unfavourable to him, he sulks. "Aw, it's a gyp," he says.

Parents who disagree on punishment put themselves in the position of risking harm to Teen no matter which they decide; for if their decision is the one more agreeable to Teen he learns the art of playing one parent against the other. This approach has proved a potent weapon in teen diplomacy.

FEET OF CLAY

THESE next two chapters are not easy to read or to write, but are important enough to demand writing and study. All through this book the ideals of youth have been emphasized. If Teen has been put on a pedestal and crowned with a halo, he is high enough to reveal more easily his feet of clay.

" To every man there openeth a high way and a low, and every man decideth the way his soul shall go."

Some things in life are beyond the control of the human will; but character is not. Two men may devote the same amount of energy to business, love, health, or enjoyment. One may get what we call the " breaks," and the other may not. But a man's rating as a human being depends on his own free will. In World War II men died on the battlefield, men died on the gallows, and men died by the firing squad. Some were criminals, some were heroes. And the free will of the victim, not even the judgment of men, determined which.

Some individuals and heads of nations suffered disaster because they were deceived by false promises of false friends. Teens just merging into adult life are in much the same position. They are drafted into adult life. Through their windows of knowledge, their senses, come many attractive offers of happiness in exchange for loyalty and service. Teens do not know why they are attracted to some things or persons and repelled by others. They rarely reflect on the consequences of yielding to an attraction or aversion, because they are not aware that they have passions stirring them to activity. Too often they become aware of some terrific force within themselves only after they have violated some teen ideal. Then they think that they are bad, and that the passion is bad, and stronger than they are.

The study of psychology has numbered eleven major passions which hold the middle ground. These passions have other forms, more or less intensive—but these eleven are commonly held standard. It will do no one any harm to think briefly about them.

Love impels us to union with and possession of the person or thing which pleases us.

Hatred makes us want to get rid of the thing that displeases us; we hate what militates against what we love.

Desire is a seeking for a loved thing that is absent.

Aversion makes us avoid approaching evil.

Joy is satisfaction that comes from a pleasure that is present.

Sadness makes us shrink from a present evil.

Courage gives us the strength to strive for union with the object we love.

Fear makes us shrink from an evil difficult to avoid.

Hope leads us to the thing loved when its possession is deemed possible.

Despair takes possession of us when attaining the object of our love is thought to be impossible.

Anger attacks what hurts us or what we love, and stirs up the desire for revenge.

The passions are not bad; actually they are the instruments for the realization of happiness, for the realization of teen ideals. But they are blind forces which tend to excess, and excess is evil. *Under the guiding force of reason passions lead unerringly to happiness.*

But passions are not weaklings; and passions allowed to go rampant may turn reason into a slave.

Even more, ideas that are not sound result in the upsurge of a particular passion.

Regulating the passions according to reason means, in practice, using one passion to moderate another. This means keeping a passion always under the strict regulation of an idea or ideal. When teens realize that they have within themselves the force necessary to control a rambunctious passion, they avoid the feeling of "being licked" before they start their battle.

Every idea that is accompanied by lively emotions and strong convictions leads into action. It is quite obvious, then, that we can judge a man's thoughts by his actions. This is particularly true when the thoughts are habitual, absorbing, fixed, for they are the real motive power of action. *Correct ideas lead to regulated passions, and to actions which are good.*

But the ideas of adults and the ideas of teens are tremendously different. Adult ideas are generally fixed, static, frozen, deeply etched by time. The ideas of teen-agers are mobile, lightly impressed, impressionable. The fixed ideas of an adult tend to determine the sway of his passions, but the influence of the passions in a teen is something that may still be moulded, still fixed, still set on the right or wrong path. It is said that the way to a man's heart is through his stomach. The way to regulate a teen's passions is through his *ideas.*

Teens occasionally are led to embrace an idea through the force of the idea itself. *But far more often they are attracted to an idea through the personality of one whom they love and trust.* The work of parents, then, must concern itself with instilling correct ideas, making them attractive, and staying eternally at their job until the right ideas become fixed in the minds of their teens.

New ideas by their very newness are strong temporarily, but any thought or idea can be driven out by a stronger thought. To teens, of course, most ideas are new; no wonder they seem unstable or fickle. Fortunately, many of the new ideas can be turned by a watchful parent into something permanently good.

But teens left to themselves have no knowledge that their ideas are influences on their actions, even on their whole future life. And too often, unfortunately, they are left to themselves. Too often they may accept even bad ideas under the appearance of good, particularly when such ideas make a strong appeal to their passions. The human intellect and will is supposed to regulate and control the passions; but intellect and will become puppets when the passions are allowed to blind them.

Left to themselves, or given the wrong guidance, teens can turn aside from their ideals, for teens have feet of clay. They are human, and under the influence of passion they can be swept into the streams of moral evil which flow from the fountainheads of pride, of envy, of anger, of avarice, of gluttony, of lust, or of sloth.

AND WINGS TO SOAR

"BUT, Father," a bewildered mother once said to me, "just how do people get ideas? I mean how does the inside of our head work?"

From the moment of birth the senses—sight, hearing, smell, taste, and touch—register impressions which are stored in the sense memory. In this sense knowledge we are the same as any other animal. For some time an infant exercises only this kind of knowledge.

When the brain is sufficiently developed, intellectual knowledge begins. This kind of knowledge only man, of all animals on earth, enjoys. The understanding of words such as *passion*, *study*, *disease*, *happiness*, *home*, *rebellion*, and *obedience* only an intellect can attain. A dog may become sick, but he will never understand the meaning of *disease*. He will never organize all dogs to fight, for instance, cancer. These are what we call general ideas, as opposed to the particular impressions made by the senses. But nothing comes into the intellect except through the senses; all through life the senses are our radar, bringing images to the intellect.

The intellect is an executive. Like a good executive, it plans activity and concerns itself not so much with doing things as with supervising them. Having evaluated an image presented by the senses, the intellect turns to its first assistant, the will.

The will is the force of power in a man. But the will has limitations. It is torn from two sides: it strives valiantly to accomplish what the intellect presents to it as necessary for the happiness of the whole man; but it often meets opposition from the senses, feelings, inclinations, passions, the whole animal part of us.

Often the intellect sees that Teen should stay at home and study, and so orders the will. But Teen's body is tired, and his senses long for rest. Perhaps a bit of swing music from the radio intrigues him. His brain finds the plugging difficult. The companionship of his fellow teenagers suggests the relaxation of the movies. This reluctance of his senses challenges the authority of his will. The fight which results in Teen's mind is never an easy one, for the forces of opposition in our own day are very strong.

It Is the Will That Makes a Man. But in addition to the very natural opposition of the senses, the will has other difficulties. The will goes into operation only on what the intellect presents to it as desirable. If the intellect is deceived, if the intellect presents evil things as desirable, the will is tricked. And it is the will that makes a man. If the intellect presents evil as desirable, the will accomplishes evil, and the whole man is harmed.

I wonder if the saddest person in the whole world isn't one whose intellect does not know where to look for happiness, nor how to judge it. Intellect and will are not self-sufficient. Their needs can be supplied only partially by other human beings, who have the same limitations. It is so clear that for complete happiness the intellect and will need One who is always right, who has no limitations—God.

Those who would like to prove that man is sufficient unto himself appeal to the great discoveries of science as a proof of man's supremacy. They like to hear the scientist lecture on the discoveries of the past, or offer radar, atomic energy, and similar present-day marvels as proof that there is no God. As people nod their heads in approval, one can count the number of heads that are bald because science cannot grow hair on them.

During the course of a lifetime, every *intellect* needs help to know what is right. The intellect can go far by itself, but the forces pushing it into error are legion. As *knowing* what is right does not always lead to *doing* what is right, the *will* constantly needs the help that only the Creator can give to overcome the forces of opposition, and to make the whole man right.

Perhaps the workings of intellect and will can best be accomplished through citing one last experience. The teen-ager, a boy, came from a rather wealthy family. He was perfectly human, and he craved happiness. But he didn't know there is a vast difference between mere pleasure and lasting happiness. He was merely conscious of an outstanding lack of happiness in himself, and of the need for something outside himself.

His senses reported many attractive things. He became curious about the ones that seemed to mean something to him. Through the senses the passions are aroused, including the passion of love, and the passion of love demands possession of the object loved. He heard about a late model convertible coupé. His companions raved about it as something very desirable, but out of the reach of all but the very rich.

His imagination gave him a glowing picture of owning the machine, so that when he finally saw the car he decided that he must have it. He never stopped for an instant to reason out *why*. Intellect and will went into conference. The one item on the agenda was how to get the machine, which his father could afford to buy, but would certainly refuse to.

His intellect saw several possible solutions. He could steal the money; that was a passing thought, rejected promptly for the very practical reason that sooner or later the theft would be discovered. He could steal the money from his father, who would never allow the matter to become public. His father's anger would be a small price to pay for the new car. But his intellect saw a new difficulty: the commandment, *Thou shalt not steal,* has binding force, even when you can get away with it. He had the courage to put the will of God before personal pleasure. He was living his religion without singing any hymns, and making an act of love of God without any feeling except disgust. He had taken a long step toward real happiness though he was too young to know it.

These eliminations left just one more way: to persuade his father to give him the money. It took several weeks, and the struggle was hard, but finally he got the object of his desire.

The thrill of possession, however, soon wore off. That is the infallible law about pleasures of the senses. Teen didn't know the essential difference between pleasure and happiness, and some people never seem to learn it. The senses experience pleasure in the process of possessing the object, and the pleasure ceases as soon as the object is fully possessed. Happiness, on the contrary, comes only from peaceful and continued possession of an object. It is a quieter thing than pleasure, and cannot exist where there is much noise and feverish activity and excitement.

Since Teen didn't know that happiness was a quiet enjoyment, he began to look elsewhere to fill the void he felt. The new car brought him a certain amount of popularity with his companions, thus directing his attention to people. He was actually on the right track, for with the animal part of us well regulated, we find most happiness in love for a person.

Among the many girls and boys who were glad to share his company and his car, Teen found one group especially congenial, and always ready for excitement. His studies began to interfere with his social life, and he began to experience an aversion to class and books. The passion of aversion or hatred is aroused against anything that seems to threaten or destroy happiness.

When circumstances forced him to look at his books, he did it with unseeing eyes, while his memory dwelt on his friends and on one girl in particular. His imagination outlined a detailed programme of future activity. He was conscious, too, that any activity would seem incomplete if his girl friend were not one of the crowd.

Continued low marks at school caused a note to be sent to his parents, and the note caused dad to have a talk with junior. After all the explanations and excuses had been brought forth and dismissed, his dad told him that the crowd he was travelling with was the cause of all his trouble. The dad stood in the doorway just before he left.

"The whole bunch of them, and the girl too," he said flatly, "wouldn't care ten cents worth for you if you didn't have the car."

"That's not true," Teen replied indignantly.

The passion of anger began to usurp the reins of common sense.

"Well, I'll tell you how true it is" the dad said. "Starting right this minute, you can't have the car until your marks are much better than they have been."

Unbidden tears came to Teen's eyes, as the passions of anger and sorrow ran riot. And for awhile the interior senses of memory and imagination fed fuel to his anger and sorrow. He sulked and became listless. Gradually the passion of sloth (the do-nothing passion) dulled the vividness of his feelings. But the very dulling process became his chief ally, and once again reason began to take over.

After a short time Teen began to see that his father was not entirely wrong about his companions. They seemed to have lost their interest in him; and he saw his erstwhile girl friend quite often with another boy who had a car like his own. The climax came when he heard the lass refer to him as a "drip."

All at once he experienced feelings strange to him, the feelings generated by the stirrings of the passion of despair. People had disappointed him in their promise of happiness. Once again his reason began to cloud up.

But his father, who had been severe before, now showed his sympathy and understanding. He came into the room one night and stood near his desk.

"Would you mind running down town to get me a couple of cigars?" he asked, throwing the key of Teen's car on the desk. "You might as well keep the key," he added, "I'm likely to lose it."

With his father to help him, he began to see that new appeals to his senses would be made all during life; that the senses can never give happiness; and that they give true pleasure only when they are regulated by reason.

And under his father's guidance he learned something more: that every human being with whom he would deal, even the girl of his dreams, would have limitations and faults.

Every teen must learn that there is no such thing in our lifetime as perfect happiness. He must be shown how to find the partial happiness which can lead him to perfect happiness. Happiness cannot be perfect so long as there is the danger, or even the possibility, of losing possession of the object loved; and the parties to the most perfect friendship, or most ideal marriage, must face eventual separation by death.

Thus, common sense leads us to the truth taught by Christ, that a man can never know complete happiness until he possesses God, a personal God, by love. And how? To that question Jesus Christ answers very simply, "If you love Me, keep My commandments." Keeping the Commandments does not exclude pleasure of the senses but regulates both. Too, keeping the Commandments regulates the passions and subjects them to reason guided unerringly by love.

This is the ultimate goal toward which parents must lead their Teen.

A FINAL WORD TO PARENTS —OR TWO

MY dear parents: Let's give full credit to the scientists whose outstanding work has put their names in the headlines. But don't envy them. Yours is the more important field of scientific activity, a field where many scientists have failed.

Generally scientists deal with materials that are dead. Generally scientists must find a way to break down the material on which they work, change it into something else, actually destroy it before they can begin to work on it, or even know it. Parents deal with *living* things.

Some scientists experiment with elements that are without feeling. And when individual experiments are failures, the scientists throw the whole mess out, or pour it back into jars for new attempts. Parents must keep and live with their failures. They aren't allowed to throw out the "whole mess" and start anew, nor even to pour it back into jars.

At best scientists carry on their investigations, endure patiently their failures, and rejoice at their successes because they are serving mankind. Parents have an infinitely higher calling—they make the mankind for whom the scientists work.

Parents are scientists, and home is their laboratory. But like everything else in our day, homes have come under the influence of change. All of the other scientists have made the best of our changing times; they have sought to improve their laboratories to bring them up to date. No doubt many scientists were attached to the ways in which their own teachers did things. Many, too, suffered great financial losses to make their laboratories more nearly perfect. But they did not sit back, hope for the best, and wait for something to happen. They investigated the work others were doing, and the equipment others were using, and brought their own laboratories up to their present state of excellence.

The succession of wars, the inventions of the movies, radio, television, automobiles, and the million other gadgets of our times have had a telling influence on our children. Too often parents have let these outside influences turn their homes into boarding-houses, good or bad, according to the amount of material comforts the parents were able to provide. Far too often parents have gone merely on the remembered experience of their own childhood, and on the methods of their own parents. Too often they have let a great scientific task rest on haphazard methods, blind wishfulness, and just pure selfish lack of interest.

There is a revolt abroad among teen-agers, a

revolt against the false glamour of the movies, shows, parties, and various forms of professional entertainment which promised them much and gave so little. They are disappointed, critical, sometimes even cynical about the attractions which draw them away from their homes.

Against every action there is a reaction. Among the youngsters I teach, and among the youngsters who come to me for spiritual guidance, there is a revolt against the influences which drew our generation away from home. There is a definite stirring in youngsters to find their happiness at home.

" Home is where you hang your hat," our generation flippantly said.

" That's not true," our youngsters are starting to say. " Home is where you find love and understanding."

Having children is essentially an animal act, having their love and their confidence is essentially a human act. Almost any couple can have children ; only hard-working parents, interested parents, planning parents, scientific parents can have the love and confidence of their children.

Parents, like other scientists, must study and learn from the successes and failures of others ; they must glean from every possible source all that will help them in the great work that has been committed to them.

There are but two parting words.

The first is this : there are many things parents

should try to achieve in raising their children, but nothing so important as winning their confidence. Before this all else falls into nothingness.

And the second is this: as I grow older, and still work with teen-agers, I see more clearly all the time—you will succeed only to the extent that you put God into your home, teaching your children to love Him and to respect His laws because they love Him.